DIGITAL AND STRATEGIC QUALITATIVE RESEARCH METHODOLOGY

First Edition

SAMUEL ADEYINKA-OJO

ISBN 979-8-89632-477-5

Contents

Preface 7

Section I
Foundations of Qualitative Research

Chapter 01 Understanding Qualitative Research 11

1.1 What is Qualitative Research? 11
1.2 Historical Evolution of Qualitative Research 11
1.3 Moments of Qualitative Research 12
1.4 Distinguishing Features of Qualitative vs. Quantitative Methods 14
1.5 Core Principles of Qualitative Inquiry 14
1.6 Summary of Section I: Foundations of Qualitative Research 15

Chapter 02 Strategic Frameworks in Qualitative Research 17

2.1 Defining Strategic Research Methodology 17
2.2 Paradigms: Positivism, Constructivism, and Pragmatism 18
2.3 Ethical Considerations in Strategic Contexts 18
2.4 Importance of Reflexivity 19
2.5 Research Philosophy 20
2.6 Qualitativc Research Approaches 21

Chapter 03 Digital Transformation in Qualitative Research 23

3.1 How Technology Shapes Research 23
3.2 Emerging Trends in Digital Data Collection 23
3.3 Digital Ethics: Privacy, Consent, and Security 24
3.4 Challenges in Adapting Traditional Methods to Digital Platforms 24

Section II
Methodologies and Techniques

Chapter 04 Data Collection Techniques 29

4.1 Interviews: Traditional, Online, and Asynchronous Methods 29
4.2 Focus Groups in the Digital Age 30
4.3 Observational Techniques: Physical and Virtual Spaces 30
4.4 Digital Surveys and Feedback Tools 31

Chapter 05 Strategic Research Planning 34

5.1 Setting Objectives and Defining Research Questions 34
5.2 Sampling Techniques: Purposive, Snowball, and Digital Sampling 35
5.3 Designing Study Protocols for Digital and Hybrid Environments 35
5.4 Addressing Bias in Strategic Research 36

Chapter 06 Analysing Qualitative Data 39

6.1 Coding and Thematic Analysis 39
6.2 Digital Tools for Analysis: NVivo, ATLAS.ti, and AI-driven Platforms 41
6.3 Content Analysis vs. Discourse Analysis 42
6.4 Visualising Qualitative Insights 43
6.5 PRISMA Checklists 44
6.6 Thematic.ai: Revolutionising Qualitative Data Analysis 49

Section III
Advanced Topics in Qualitative Research

Chapter 07 Digital Ethnography 55

7.1 Conducting Ethnography in Online Communities 55
7.2 Netnography: Researching Social Media Spaces 56
7.3 Ethical Dilemmas in Digital Ethnography 56

Chapter 08 Case Study Methodology 59

8.1 Designing a Qualitative Case Study 59
8.2 Integrating Digital Evidence in Case Studies 60
8.3 Strategic Case Analysis for Policy and Practice 60

Chapter 09 Mixed Methods and Triangulation 62

9.1 Blending Qualitative and Quantitative Approaches 62
9.2 Using Triangulation to Enhance Credibility 63
9.3 Strategic Applications of Mixed Methods Research 63

Chapter 10 Advanced Digital Tools and Techniques 66

10.1 Using Social Media Analytics for Research 66
10.2 Mining Digital Data: Challenges and Opportunities 67
10.3 AI and Machine Learning in Qualitative Research 67

Section IV
Applications and Implications

Chapter 11 Practical Applications in Various Disciplines 73

11.1 Marketing and Consumer Research 73
11.2 Education and Pedagogical Research 74
11.3 Healthcare and Public Policy Studies 74
11.4 Social Justice and Advocacy Research 75

Chapter 12 Reporting and Presenting Qualitative Findings 77

12.1 Writing Reports for Academic and Strategic Audiences 77
12.2 Visualising Findings: Infographics, Dashboards, and Multimedia 78
12.3 Publishing in the Digital Era 78

Chapter 13 Future of Qualitative Research 81

13.1 Trends Shaping the Future of Digital Qualitative Methods 81
13.2 Addressing the Challenges of Digital Research 82
13.3 Towards a More Inclusive and Global Research Framework 83

Section V
Computer-Assisted Qualitative Data Analysis Software (CAQDAS)

Chapter 14 Software for Qualitative Data Analysis 89

14.1 NVivo v.14 (2023 Version) Step-by-Step Applications 89
14.2 QDA Miner 94
14.3 Taguette 94
14.4 Thematic.ai 95
14.5 MAXQDA 95

14.6 ATLAS.ti....95
14.7 QualCoder....96
14.8 HyperRESEARCH....96
14.9 Content Analysis....96
14.10 Qualtrics XM....97
14.11 HubSpot....97
14.12 Text Analysis....97
14.13 Weft Qualitative Data Analysis....98
14.14 RQDA....98
14.15 F4analysis....98

Chapter 15 Extended Qualitative Research Methodologies....100

15.1 Means-End Chain Theory....100
15.2 Laddering Technique....101
15.3 Kelly Repertory Grid....102
15.4 Online Qualitative Methods....104

Chapter 16 Preference of Qualitative Research Methodology Over Quantitative and Mixed Methods....106

16.1 Qualitative Versus Quantitative Research....106
16.2 Qualitative Versus Mixed Methods....107
16.3 Strengths and Weaknesses of Qualitative Research Methodology....108
16.4 Strategies to Address Weaknesses....109
16.5 Examples of Well-Known Qualitative Research Projects....109

About the Author....*113*

Preface

Preface to Digital and Strategic Qualitative Research Methodology

This preface of Digital and Strategic Qualitative Research Methodology serves as an introduction, laying the foundation for understanding the scope, audience, and unique contributions of the textbook. It sets the tone for the content, highlights its relevance, and provides an overview of its structure and key features. By catering to a diverse audience, emphasising digital innovation, and connecting qualitative research to strategic applications, the textbook positions itself as a forward-thinking resource for learners and professionals alike.

Introduction, Purpose and Relevance of the Textbook

The textbook is designed to address the evolving landscape of qualitative research in the Digital Age, where technological advancements and strategic considerations have become integral to research methodologies. While rooted in classical qualitative research principles, the book emphasises integrating digital tools and strategies to enhance data collection, analysis, and presentation. The text explores how digital advancements, such as artificial intelligence (AI), machine learning, and social media analytics, are reshaping qualitative research. The book caters to researchers across diverse fields, including social sciences, marketing, healthcare, education, and policy studies.

Synopsis and Structure of the Book

The textbook is structured to provide a comprehensive yet accessible exploration of digital and strategic qualitative research. The book is divided into five sections, each addressing a critical aspect of qualitative research: [a] foundations of qualitative research: understanding qualitative research, strategic frameworks in qualitative research, and digital transformation in qualitative research; [b] methodologies and techniques: data collection techniques, strategic research planning, and analysing qualitative data; [c] advanced topics in qualitative research: digital ethnography, case study methodology, mixed methods and triangulation, and advanced digital tools and techniques; [d] applications and implications: practical applications in various disciplines, reporting and presenting qualitative findings, future of qualitative research, and [e] computer-assisted qualitative data analysis software (CAQDAS): software for qualitative data analysis, extended qualitative research methodologies, and preference of qualitative research methodology over quantitative and mixed methods.

SECTION I

Foundations of Qualitative Research

Chapter 01

Understanding Qualitative Research

1.1 What is Qualitative Research?
1.2 Historical Evolution of Qualitative Research
1.3 Moments of Qualitative Research
1.4 Distinguishing Features of Qualitative vs Quantitative Methods
1.5 Core Principles of Qualitative Inquiry,
1.6 Summary of Section 1: Foundation of Qualitative Research.

1.1 What is Qualitative Research?

Qualitative research is a methodological approach that seeks to understand the complexities of human experiences, behaviours, and interactions. It focuses on exploring meanings, perspectives, and the context in which phenomena occur (Creswell & Poth, 2018). Unlike quantitative research, which relies on numerical data, qualitative research emphasises textual or narrative data to provide in-depth insights. This approach is often used in disciplines like sociology, psychology, education, and health sciences, where understanding subjective experiences is crucial (Denzin & Lincoln, 2018).

Key characteristics of qualitative research include its exploratory nature, flexibility, and reliance on smaller, purposive samples rather than large, random ones. Researchers often use open-ended questions, interviews, focus groups, and ethnographic observations to gather data (Patton, 2015). The ultimate goal is to generate a nuanced understanding rather than to generalise findings to broader populations.

In today's Digital Age, qualitative research has expanded to include virtual ethnography, online interviews, and social media analysis, broadening its scope and applicability (Hine, 2015).

1.2 Historical Evolution of Qualitative Research

The roots of qualitative research can be traced back to philosophical traditions such as interpretivism and phenomenology. Interpretivism, introduced by thinkers like Max Weber, emphasised understanding social action from the actor's perspective (Weber, 1978). Similarly, phenomenology, championed by Edmund Husserl, focused on the lived experiences of individuals to uncover the essence of phenomena (van Manen, 1990).

Early qualitative research was heavily influenced by anthropology and sociology. Ethnographic studies, such as Bronisław Malinowski's work on the Trobriand Islanders, showcased the value of immersive fieldwork in understanding cultures (Malinowski, 1922). In sociology, the Chicago School in the early 20th century pioneered urban ethnography, with landmark studies such as *The Polish Peasant in Europe and America* by Thomas and Znaniecki (1918).

Post-World War II, qualitative research gained momentum in diverse disciplines, driven by critiques of positivism's limitations in capturing the complexity of human behaviour. Scholars like Clifford Geertz emphasised "thick description" to provide rich contextual detail (Geertz, 1973). The feminist movement in the 1970s further contributed to qualitative research by highlighting marginalised voices and advocating for participatory approaches (Reinharz, 1992).

In recent decades, advancements in digital technology have transformed qualitative research, enabling innovative methods like digital ethnography, social media analytics, and AI-driven data analysis (Hesse-Biber & Griffin, 2013).

1.3 Moments of Qualitative Research

In the qualitative research study, list and explain the moments of qualitative research from 1900 to 2024. Provide all the periods or phases and years. Include in-text citations and a reference list using APA style.

The development of qualitative research from 1900 to 2024 can be understood through various "moments," or phases, that reflect its evolution in theory, methodology, and practice. These moments, outlined by scholars like Denzin and Lincoln (2018), showcase how qualitative research has adapted to historical, social, and intellectual shifts. Below is an overview of the key moments in qualitative research:

1. The Traditional Period (1900–1950s).

This phase focused on ethnographic fieldwork influenced by anthropology and sociology. Researchers aimed to capture "objective" cultural truths using participant observation and interviews. The emphasis was on neutrality and realist representation. For example, Malinowski's **Argonauts of the Western Pacific** (1922) epitomises this era's methodological rigour.

2. The Modernist or Golden Age (1950–1970)

This period saw the expansion of qualitative methods with a focus on validity and reliability. Researchers explored grounded theory (e.g., Glaser & Strauss, 1967), enhancing the systematic development of theories based on data. Qualitative work was also influenced by the positivist traditions, striving for rigour akin to quantitative methods.

3. The Blurred Genres Phase (1970–1986)

Qualitative research diversified as interdisciplinary methods emerged. Scholars like Geertz (1973) emphasised thick description, blending interpretive anthropology with social science inquiry. Research began incorporating literary and artistic forms, and the lines between genres blurred, leading to innovative narratives and reflexivity in research practices.

4. The Crisis of Representation (1986–1990)

This moment arose from critiques of objectivity and representation in qualitative research. Postmodernist influences led to questions about whose voices are heard and how power dynamics shape knowledge production (Clifford & Marcus, 1986). Researchers embraced reflexivity, acknowledging their influence on the research process.

5. The Postmodern Period (1990–1995)

Postmodernism further challenged traditional notions of truth and realism. Researchers adopted more experimental writing styles and methodologies, recognising the constructed nature of knowledge. This phase embraced narrative, discourse analysis, and other methods that highlighted subjectivity and multiple realities.

6. The Post-Experimental Inquiry Phase (1995–2000)

Innovations in this phase included performative and arts-based research approaches. Researchers experimented with multimedia formats, including poetry, theatre, and film, to present findings, expanding how knowledge could be communicated and experienced.

7. The Methodologically Contested Present (2000–2010)

Debates over methodological rigour, ethics, and representation marked this phase. The rise of mixed methods research sought to bridge qualitative and quantitative paradigms. Researchers examined how digital tools could influence qualitative inquiry.

8. The Global and Decolonizing Turn (2010–2024)

The most recent moment emphasises inclusivity, equity, and decolonisation in research practices. Scholars critique Western-centric paradigms and prioritise indigenous methodologies and community-based participatory research (Smith, 2012). Digital technologies, such as AI and big data, have also expanded possibilities for qualitative research.

References

Clifford, J., & Marcus, G. E. (Eds.). (1986). *Writing culture: The poetics and politics of ethnography*. University of California Press.

Denzin, N. K., & Lincoln, Y. S. (2018). *The Sage handbook of qualitative research* (5th ed.). Sage Publications.

Geertz, C. (1973). *The interpretation of cultures*. Basic Books.

Glaser, B., & Strauss, A. (1967). *The discovery of grounded theory: Strategies for qualitative research*. Aldine Publishing.

1.4 Distinguishing Features of Qualitative vs. Quantitative Methods

While both qualitative and quantitative research aim to generate knowledge, their approaches differ significantly.

Nature of Data:

- Qualitative research relies on non-numerical data such as interviews, narratives, and field notes.
- Quantitative research uses numerical data and statistical methods to test hypotheses (Bryman, 2016).

Research Objectives:

- Qualitative research explores "how" and "why" questions to understand processes and meanings.
- Quantitative research addresses "what" questions to measure variables and test relationships.

Sample Size and Selection:

- Qualitative studies use smaller, purposive samples to gain depth.
- Quantitative studies involve larger, random samples to ensure generalizability.

Analytical Techniques:

- Qualitative analysis includes coding, thematic analysis, and discourse analysis to interpret data.
- Quantitative analysis employs statistical tools like regression and correlation (Creswell, 2014).

Strengths and Limitations:

- Qualitative methods excel in contextual understanding but may lack generalizability.
- Quantitative methods provide broad applicability but often miss nuanced insights.

The integration of both methods in mixed methods research is increasingly recognised as a way to leverage the strengths of each (Tashakkori & Teddlie, 2010).

1.5 Core Principles of Qualitative Inquiry

Qualitative research is guided by several core principles that ensure its rigour and relevance:

1. Contextual Understanding:

Qualitative research prioritises understanding phenomena within their social, cultural, and historical contexts. This principle aligns with the interpretivist paradigm, emphasising the importance of situating findings within real-world settings (Denzin & Lincoln, 2018).

2. Participant-Centred Approach:

Participants' voices and perspectives are central to qualitative research. Methods like in-depth interviews and focus groups allow participants to share their experiences, ensuring their lived realities are authentically represented (Patton, 2015).

3. Reflexivity:

Researchers acknowledge their biases and their influence on the research process. Reflexivity involves critically examining how personal beliefs, values, and positions affect data interpretation (Finlay, 2002).

4. Iterative Process:

Qualitative research is inherently flexible and iterative. Researchers often revise research questions and methods based on emerging data and insights (Charmaz, 2014).

5. Credibility and Trustworthiness:

Strategies such as triangulation, member checking, and thick description enhance the credibility of qualitative findings. Unlike quantitative reliability, qualitative rigour focuses on ensuring the authenticity and resonance of interpretations (Lincoln & Guba, 1985).

6. Ethical Responsibility:

Ethical considerations are integral to qualitative research. Researchers must ensure informed consent, maintain confidentiality, and minimise harm to participants (Orb, Eisenhauer, & Wynaden, 2001).

1.6 Summary of Section I: Foundations of Qualitative Research

This chapter established a foundational understanding of qualitative research, outlining its definition, evolution, distinguishing features, and guiding principles. Qualitative research is a vital methodology for exploring complex human phenomena, providing depth and context often unattainable through quantitative methods. Its historical evolution highlights its adaptability and relevance across disciplines, from anthropology to healthcare. The distinction between qualitative and quantitative methods underscores their complementary nature, with qualitative research excelling in understanding meanings and processes. Finally, the core principles of qualitative inquiry, including reflexivity and contextual understanding, ensure its rigour and ethical integrity. Together, these elements form the bedrock of qualitative research, setting the stage for its application in diverse fields.

References

Bryman, A. (2016). *Social research methods* (5th ed.). Oxford University Press.

Charmaz, K. (2014). *Constructing grounded theory* (2nd ed.). Sage.

Creswell, J. W. (2014). *Research design: Qualitative, quantitative, and mixed methods approaches* (4th ed.). Sage.

Creswell, J. W., & Poth, C. N. (2018). *Qualitative inquiry and research design: Choosing among five approaches* (4th ed.). Sage.

Denzin, N. K., & Lincoln, Y. S. (2018). *The Sage handbook of qualitative research* (5th ed.). Sage.

Finlay, L. (2002). Negotiating the swamp: The opportunity and challenge of reflexivity in research practice. *Qualitative Research*, 2(2), 209–230. https://doi.org/10.1177/146879410200200205

Geertz, C. (1973). *The interpretation of cultures: Selected essays*. Basic Books.

Hesse-Biber, S., & Griffin, A. J. (2013). Internet-mediated technologies and mixed methods research: Problems and prospects. *Journal of Mixed Methods Research*, 7(1), 43–61. https://doi.org/10.1177/1558689812451791

Hine, C. (2015). *Ethnography for the internet: Embedded, embodied, and everyday*. Bloomsbury Academic.

Lincoln, Y. S., & Guba, E. G. (1985). *Naturalistic inquiry*. Sage.

Malinowski, B. (1922). *Argonauts of the Western Pacific*. Routledge.

Orb, A., Eisenhauer, L., & Wynaden, D. (2001). Ethics in qualitative research. *Journal of Nursing Scholarship*, 33(1), 93–96. https://doi.org/10.1111/j.1547-5069.2001.00093.x

Patton, M. Q. (2015). *Qualitative research and evaluation methods* (4th ed.). Sage.

Reinharz, S. (1992). *Feminist methods in social research*. Oxford University Press.

Tashakkori, A., & Teddlie, C. (2010). *Mixed methods in social and behavioral research* (2nd ed.). Sage.

van Manen, M. (1990). *Researching lived experience: Human science for an action-sensitive pedagogy*. State University of New York Press.

Weber, M. (1978). *Economy and society*. University of California Press.

Chapter 02

Strategic Frameworks in Qualitative Research

2.1 Defining Strategic Research Methodology.
2.2 Paradigms: Positivism, Constructivism, and Pragmatism.
2.3 Ethical Considerations in Strategic Contexts.
2.4 Importance of Reflexivity.
2.5 Research Philosophy: Ontology, Epistemology, Axiology, Methodology, and Rhetoric
2.6 Qualitative Research Approaches: Grounded Theory, Ethnography, Phenomenology,
2.7 Case Study and Narrative Research

2.1 Defining Strategic Research Methodology

Strategic research methodology refers to the systematic, deliberate approach to designing and conducting research in alignment with specific goals or objectives. In qualitative research, the strategic aspect emphasises the alignment between research questions, methods, and intended outcomes, ensuring that the research contributes meaningfully to the understanding of complex phenomena (Patton, 2015).

A strategic approach in qualitative research involves careful planning, the use of appropriate theoretical frameworks, and adaptive methodologies to address dynamic contexts. This method often integrates iterative processes, where initial findings inform subsequent phases of research (Tracy, 2020).

For example, in health studies, researchers adopting a strategic methodology might design their inquiry to address policy gaps while actively engaging stakeholders throughout the process. This ensures that the research not only generates insights but also drives actionable change (Creswell & Poth, 2018).

In a digital context, strategic methodologies also consider how technological tools can enhance data collection, analysis, and dissemination. For instance, the use of social media analytics in understanding public sentiment represents a strategic alignment of tools with research objectives (Hesse-Biber & Griffin, 2013).

2.2 Paradigms: Positivism, Constructivism, and Pragmatism

Research paradigms serve as overarching frameworks that guide the methodologies, epistemologies, and ontologies underpinning a study. The strategic selection of a paradigm is crucial in qualitative research as it shapes the study's design and interpretation.

Positivism

Positivism asserts that reality is objective and can be observed, measured, and understood through scientific inquiry. In qualitative research, however, positivism plays a limited role due to its reliance on measurable data and structured methods (Bryman, 2016). When applied, positivism often informs studies seeking to establish causal relationships or test predetermined theories.

Constructivism

Constructivism, rooted in interpretivist traditions, emphasises that reality is socially constructed and subjective. This paradigm underlies most qualitative research, focusing on how individuals interpret and ascribe meaning to their experiences (Denzin & Lincoln, 2018). Constructivist studies employ flexible and participatory methods, such as ethnography or grounded theory, to uncover nuanced insights. For example, a constructivist approach might explore how cultural values shape perceptions of health interventions, prioritising the voices and perspectives of study participants (Charmaz, 2014).

Pragmatism

Pragmatism bridges positivism and constructivism by emphasising the practical application of research. This paradigm focuses on problem-solving, often integrating mixed methods to address complex research questions (Creswell & Plano Clark, 2017). Pragmatism is particularly relevant in strategic qualitative research, where the goal is to generate actionable knowledge. For instance, a pragmatic approach might involve using interviews to explore user experiences while simultaneously analysing usage data to improve digital applications. The selection of a paradigm should align with the research objectives, ensuring methodological coherence and philosophical consistency (Tashakkori & Teddlie, 2010).

2.3 Ethical Considerations in Strategic Contexts

Ethical considerations are foundational to all research but take on heightened significance in strategic qualitative research due to its focus on human experiences and interactions. Researchers must navigate ethical challenges carefully to protect participants' rights and maintain research integrity.

Informed Consent

Obtaining informed consent ensures participants understand the purpose, methods, and implications of the research. In strategic contexts where power dynamics or sensitive topics may be involved, informed consent should be an ongoing process, revisited at key stages of the study (Orb et al., 2001).

Confidentiality and Anonymity

Protecting participants' identities is critical, particularly in strategic studies involving sensitive data. Researchers must use pseudonyms or anonymise data to prevent breaches of confidentiality, especially when disseminating findings in public or policy forums (Patton, 2015).

Cultural Sensitivity

Strategic qualitative research often involves diverse populations, requiring cultural competence to ensure respectful and inclusive practices. For example, researchers studying indigenous communities must adapt their methodologies to align with cultural norms and values, incorporating participatory approaches where possible (Smith, 2012).

Navigating Power Dynamics

Strategic research often involves stakeholders with varying levels of power, such as policymakers, practitioners, and community members. Researchers must balance these dynamics, ensuring that marginalised voices are prioritised and that findings are not co-opted by dominant groups (Tracy, 2020).

Digital Ethics

In the Digital Age, strategic research increasingly involves online environments. Ethical challenges include ensuring data privacy, obtaining consent for online interactions, and addressing the potential biases of algorithm-driven analyses (Hesse-Biber & Griffin, 2013).

By adhering to ethical guidelines and prioritising participant well-being, researchers enhance the credibility and impact of their strategic studies.

2.4 Importance of Reflexivity

Reflexivity is the process by which researchers critically examine their positionality, assumptions, and influence on the research process. In strategic qualitative research, reflexivity is essential for ensuring methodological rigour and ethical integrity (Finlay, 2002).

Personal Reflexivity

Personal reflexivity involves acknowledging how a researcher's background, values, and experiences shape the study. For instance, a health researcher exploring patient experiences may need to reflect on how their professional role influences interactions with participants (Charmaz, 2014).

Epistemological Reflexivity

Epistemological reflexivity examines the assumptions underlying the research design and methodology. Researchers must consider how their chosen paradigm and methods influence the types of knowledge generated and the study's broader implications (Bryman, 2016).

Methodological Reflexivity

Methodological reflexivity involves evaluating the strengths and limitations of the research methods used. For example, a researcher conducting virtual interviews might reflect on how the lack of face-to-face interaction affects data quality and participant engagement (Tracy, 2020).

Collaborative Reflexivity

In strategic contexts, researchers often collaborate with stakeholders. Reflexivity in these partnerships ensures that power imbalances are addressed and diverse perspectives are meaningfully integrated into the research process (Smith, 2012).

Reflexivity is not a one-time exercise but an ongoing commitment to transparency and accountability throughout the research journey. By engaging in reflexive practices, researchers enhance the validity and trustworthiness of their findings, contributing to more robust and impactful qualitative research (Lincoln & Guba, 1985).

2.5 Research Philosophy

These include **ontology**, **epistemology**, **axiology**, **methodology**, and **rhetorical**.

[a]. Ontology - The nature of reality (Denzin & Lincoln, 2005).

[b]. Epistemology - Is the theory of knowledge, which asks the main questions of 'what is knowledge' and how do we produce it, or how do we know the world? It deals with the relationship between the knower (researcher or inquirer) and the known (knowable) or what can be known.

[c]. Methodology - Is concerned with the procedures for understanding the world and how the researcher or inquirer goes about finding out knowledge. Methodology is the justification for using a particular research method.

[ci]. **Method:** is simply a **research** tool, a component of **research** – say, for example, a qualitative **method** such as interviews (in-depth, focus, etc.)

[d]. **Axiology** - the fundamental goal of research, including values and ethics. In other words, axiological (i.e. values and biases).

[e]. **Rhetorical** - Is viewed as the choice of language used by the researcher in the written text, and "words such as understanding, discover, and meaning form the glossary of emerging qualitative terms". In other words, Rhetorical (choice of language) assumptions of the researcher used in the inquiry paradigm.

2.6 Qualitative Research Approaches

These are grounded theory, ethnography, phenomenology, case study, and narrative research Creswell and Poth (2018, pp. 65-106).

[a]. **Grounded theory** - Grounded theory (GT) was developed by (Glaser & Strauss, 1967) who felt that theories used in research were often inappropriate and ill-suited for participants under study. GT is to generate or discover a theory, a "unified theoretical explanation" (Corbin & Strauss, 2007, p. 107).

[b]. **Ethnography** - Describe and interpret a culture-sharing group. It describes and interprets the shared patterns of culture of a group.

[c]: **Phenomenology** - Phenomenological study describes the common meaning for several individuals of their lived experiences of a concept or a phenomenon. It describes the essence of a lived phenomenon or event.

[d]. **Case Study** - Qualitative Case Study as an intensive, holistic description and analysis of a single instance or event, phenomenon, or social unit (Merriam, 1998). Develop an in-depth description and analysis of a case or multiple cases.

[e]. **Narrative Research** - Explore the life of an individual. Tell stories of individual experiences.

References

Bryman, A. (2016). *Social research methods* (5th ed.). Oxford University Press.

Charmaz, K. (2014). *Constructing grounded theory* (2nd ed.). Sage.

Creswell, J. W., & Plano Clark, V. L. (2017). *Designing and conducting mixed methods research* (3rd ed.). Sage.

Creswell, J. W., & Poth, C. N. (2018). *Qualitative inquiry and research design: Choosing among five approaches* (4th ed.). Sage.

Denzin, N. K., & Lincoln, Y. S. (2018). *The Sage handbook of qualitative research* (5th ed.). Sage.Denzin, N.K. & Lincoln, Y.S. (2005). *Handbook of qualitative research (3rd ed.).* Thousands Oaks, CA: Sage Publications Inc.

Finlay, L. (2002). Negotiating the swamp: The opportunity and challenge of reflexivity in research practice. *Qualitative Research*, 2(2), 209–230. https://doi.org/10.1177/146879410200200205

Hesse-Biber, S., & Griffin, A. J. (2013). Internet-mediated technologies and mixed methods research: Problems and prospects. *Journal of Mixed Methods Research*, 7(1), 43–61. https://doi.org/10.1177/1558689812451791

Lincoln, Y. S., & Guba, E. G. (1985). *Naturalistic inquiry*. Sage.

Orb, A., Eisenhauer, L., & Wynaden, D. (2001). Ethics in qualitative research. *Journal of Nursing Scholarship*, 33(1), 93–96. https://doi.org/10.1111/j.1547-5069.2001.00093.x

Patton, M. Q. (2015). *Qualitative research and evaluation methods* (4th ed.). Sage.

Smith, L. T. (2012). *Decolonizing methodologies: Research and Indigenous peoples* (2nd ed.). Zed Books.

Tashakkori, A., & Teddlie, C. (2010). *Mixed methods in social and behavioral research* (2nd ed.). Sage.

Tracy, S. J. (2020). *Qualitative research methods: Collecting evidence, crafting analysis, communicating impact* (2nd ed.). Wiley.

Chapter 03

Digital Transformation in Qualitative Research

3.1 How Technology Shapes Research.
3.2 Emerging Trends in Digital Data Collection.
3.3 Digital Ethics: Privacy, Consent, and Security
3.4 Challenges in Adapting Traditional Methods to Digital Platforms.

3.1 How Technology Shapes Research

Technology has revolutionised qualitative research by expanding the ways researchers collect, analyse, and interpret data. Digital tools such as video conferencing platforms, transcription software, and qualitative data analysis software (e.g., NVivo and Atlas.ti) have made the research process more efficient and accessible (Silver & Lewins, 2014). For instance, interviews can now be conducted remotely, eliminating geographical barriers and increasing the diversity of study participants (Deakin & Wakefield, 2014).

Technology also facilitates the use of multimedia data, such as videos and social media posts, which can be analysed for richer insights. These innovations allow researchers to examine real-time interactions, offering dynamic perspectives on phenomena (Paulus, Lester, & Dempster, 2014). However, the integration of digital tools also demands a shift in researcher skillsets, requiring technical proficiency and adaptability to new platforms.

3.2 Emerging Trends in Digital Data Collection

Digital data collection methods are evolving rapidly. Social media platforms like Twitter and Facebook, alongside messaging apps, have become rich sources of qualitative data, enabling researchers to explore online communities and discourse (Sloan & Quan-Haase, 2017). Virtual focus groups, facilitated by tools like Zoom, offer a cost-effective way to gather group-level insights without requiring physical presence (Stewart & Shamdasani, 2017).

Moreover, mobile ethnography is gaining traction, where participants use mobile devices to document their experiences through photos, videos, and text (Pink et al., 2016). This trend provides more authentic data, as participants capture their experiences in natural settings.

Big data analytics, another emerging trend, allows qualitative researchers to process and analyse large datasets, such as customer reviews or social media content, providing deeper insights into societal trends (Uprichard, 2013).

3.3 Digital Ethics: Privacy, Consent, and Security

The digital transformation of qualitative research raises critical ethical considerations. Protecting participant privacy is a significant challenge when working with online data, especially on public platforms. Researchers must navigate complex issues of informed consent, particularly when dealing with data that participants might not perceive as private (Markham & Buchanan, 2012).

Data security is another concern, as researchers are responsible for safeguarding sensitive information from breaches or misuse. Ethical guidelines, such as those from the Association of Internet Researchers (AoIR), provide frameworks for addressing these challenges. They emphasise transparency, participant autonomy, and the need to adapt traditional ethical principles to the digital context (Buchanan, 2017).

3.4 Challenges in Adapting Traditional Methods to Digital Platforms

Adapting traditional qualitative methods to digital platforms presents several challenges. First, establishing rapport with participants in virtual settings can be difficult due to the lack of physical cues and body language (Deakin & Wakefield, 2014). Second, digital tools may exclude participants who lack access to technology or have limited digital literacy, introducing potential biases in the data (Roberts et al., 2021).

Third, the sheer volume of data available online can overwhelm researchers, necessitating robust strategies for data management and analysis (Sloan & Quan-Haase, 2017). Finally, the fast-paced evolution of technology requires researchers to stay updated on new tools and methodologies, which can be resource-intensive. Addressing these challenges demands a balanced approach that integrates technological advancements with the core principles of qualitative research.

References

Buchanan, E. (2017). Internet research ethics: Past, present, and future. In N. Fielding, R. M. Lee, & G. Blank (Eds.), *The SAGE handbook of online research methods* (2nd ed., pp. 21–37). SAGE Publications.

Deakin, H., & Wakefield, K. (2014). Skype interviewing: Reflections of two PhD researchers. *Qualitative Research, 14*(5), 603–616. https://doi.org/10.1177/1468794113488126

Markham, A., & Buchanan, E. (2012). Ethical decision-making and Internet research: Recommendations from the AoIR ethics working committee. Retrieved from https://aoir.org/reports/ethics2.pdf.

Paulus, T., Lester, J., & Dempster, P. (2014). *Digital tools for qualitative research.* SAGE Publications.

Pink, S., Horst, H., Postill, J., Hjorth, L., Lewis, T., & Tacchi, J. (2016). *Digital ethnography: Principles and practice.* SAGE Publications.

Roberts, J. K., Pavlakis, A. E., & Richards, M. P. (2021). It's more complicated than it seems: Virtual qualitative research in the COVID-19 era. *International Journal of Qualitative Methods, 20*, 1–13. https://doi.org/10.1177/16094069211002959

Silver, C., & Lewins, A. (2014). *Using software in qualitative research: A step-by-step guide.* SAGE Publications.

Sloan, L., & Quan-Haase, A. (2017). *The SAGE handbook of social media research methods.* SAGE Publications.

Stewart, D. W., & Shamdasani, P. N. (2017). *Focus groups: Theory and practice* (3rd ed.). SAGE Publications.

Uprichard, E. (2013). Big data, little questions? *Discover Society.* Retrieved from https://www.discoversociety.org

SECTION II

Methodologies and Techniques

Chapter 04

Data Collection Techniques

4.1 Interviews: Traditional, Online, and Asynchronous Methods.
4.2 Focus Groups in the Digital Age.
4.3 Observational Techniques: Physical and Virtual Spaces.
4.4 Digital Surveys and Feedback Tools.

Data collection is the cornerstone of research, offering insights into phenomena, behaviour, and perceptions. With advancements in digital technology, traditional methods of data collection are being transformed, enabling researchers to gather data more efficiently and inclusively. This chapter examines the methodologies of interviews, focus groups, observational techniques, and digital surveys, highlighting their applications in both physical and virtual contexts.

4.1 Interviews: Traditional, Online, and Asynchronous Methods

Traditional Interviews

Face-to-face interviews remain a cornerstone of qualitative research, allowing researchers to build rapport, observe non-verbal cues, and explore topics in-depth. These interviews are typically conducted in controlled environments, enabling detailed interactions between participants and researchers (Kvale & Brinkmann, 2015). Despite their advantages, traditional interviews can be time-consuming and logistically challenging, particularly when participants are geographically dispersed (Gill et al., 2008).

Online Interviews

The rise of digital platforms has revolutionised interview methods. Tools like Zoom, Microsoft Teams, and Skype allow researchers to conduct interviews remotely, breaking geographical barriers and enabling real-time data collection (Deakin & Wakefield, 2014). Online interviews are particularly valuable for accessing marginalised or hard-to-reach populations. However, technical issues, lack of physical cues, and participants' varying digital literacy can pose challenges (Seitz, 2016).

Asynchronous Interviews

Asynchronous interviews, conducted through email or messaging platforms, offer participants the flexibility to respond at their convenience. This method is beneficial for participants with busy schedules or those who prefer written communication (O'Connor et al., 2008). While asynchronous interviews may lack immediacy and spontaneous interaction, they allow for thoughtful and reflective responses, making them suitable for sensitive topics or participants with communication barriers.

4.2 Focus Groups in the Digital Age

Focus groups, traditionally conducted in-person, have evolved with digital technology. These group discussions are designed to explore collective views, stimulate discussion, and identify patterns in perceptions (Krueger & Casey, 2015).

Traditional Focus Groups

Face-to-face focus groups are valued for their ability to generate dynamic interactions, with participants building on each other's responses. However, logistical issues, such as scheduling and travel, can limit their feasibility (Morgan, 1997).

Virtual Focus Groups

Virtual focus groups conducted on platforms like Zoom or Google Meet address many logistical challenges, offering flexibility and cost efficiency. They enable researchers to reach a wider audience, including geographically dispersed participants (Stewart & Shamdasani, 2017). However, virtual settings may inhibit natural interaction, as participants might struggle with overlapping speech or technical difficulties (Abrams et al., 2015).

Hybrid Focus Groups

Hybrid approaches, combining in-person and virtual participation, have gained popularity. This method accommodates participants with varying availability and preferences, ensuring inclusivity. Effective moderation is crucial to manage the dynamics between in-person and virtual participants (Gibbs, 2012).

4.3 Observational Techniques: Physical and Virtual Spaces

Observation is a foundational technique in qualitative research, providing insights into behaviour, context, and interactions.

Physical Observation

In-person observation, conducted in natural settings, allows researchers to capture authentic behaviours and environmental context. Ethnographic methods, such as participant observation, are particularly effective for studying cultures and communities (Hammersley & Atkinson, 2019). Challenges include observer bias and the difficulty of remaining unobtrusive in the field (Angrosino, 2007).

Virtual Observation

Virtual observation involves studying behaviours and interactions in digital spaces, such as social media platforms, online forums, and virtual worlds. This method is valuable for examining online communities and digital behaviour (Garcia et al., 2009). Tools like NVivo and ATLAS.ti facilitate the analysis of digital interactions. Ethical considerations, including privacy and consent, are critical in virtual observation (Markham & Buchanan, 2012).

Comparative Advantages

While physical observation offers richness and contextual depth, virtual observation provides access to global, real-time data. Combining both approaches can yield comprehensive insights, especially when studying phenomena that traverse digital and physical realms (Murthy, 2008).

4.4 Digital Surveys and Feedback Tools

Digital surveys have become a staple in both qualitative and quantitative research, offering scalability, efficiency, and flexibility.

Advantages of Digital Surveys

Digital surveys, distributed via platforms like Google Forms, SurveyMonkey, and Qualtrics, enable researchers to collect data from large populations quickly. Features such as branching logic and multimedia integration enhance the survey experience and allow for more nuanced data collection (Wright, 2005).

Types of Digital Surveys

- **Self-administered Surveys:** Participants complete these surveys independently, offering convenience and reducing interviewer bias (Dillman et al., 2014).
- **Mobile Surveys**: Optimised for smartphones, these surveys cater to participants who primarily use mobile devices, increasing response rates (Mavletova & Couper, 2015).
- **Interactive Surveys**: Incorporating gamification or interactive elements, these surveys enhance engagement and data quality (Harms et al., 2015).

Feedback Tools

Digital feedback tools, such as online comment boxes and real-time polls, provide quick insights and foster participant engagement. Social media listening tools also serve as indirect feedback mechanisms, capturing spontaneous opinions and trends (Tuten & Solomon, 2017).

Limitations and Challenges

Despite their advantages, digital surveys face limitations, such as non-response bias and issues with data quality. Researchers must also address accessibility and digital literacy to ensure inclusivity (Couper, 2017).

References

Abrams, K. M., Wang, Z., Song, Y. J., & Galindo-Gonzalez, S. (2015). Data richness trade-offs between face-to-face, online audiovisual, and online text-only focus groups. *Social Science Computer Review, 33*(1), 80–96. https://doi.org/10.1177/0894439313519733

Angrosino, M. (2007). *Doing ethnographic and observational research.* SAGE Publications.

Couper, M. P. (2017). New developments in survey data collection. *Annual Review of Sociology, 43*, 121–145. https://doi.org/10.1146/annurev-soc-060116-053613

Dillman, D. A., Smyth, J. D., & Christian, L. M. (2014). *Internet, phone, mail, and mixed-mode surveys: The tailored design method* (4th ed.). Wiley.

Garcia, A. C., Standlee, A. I., Bechkoff, J., & Yan, C. (2009). Ethnographic approaches to the Internet and computer-mediated communication. *Journal of Contemporary Ethnography, 38*(1), 52–84. https://doi.org/10.1177/0891241607310839

Gibbs, G. R. (2012). *The analysis of qualitative data.* SAGE Publications.

Gill, P., Stewart, K., Treasure, E., & Chadwick, B. (2008). Methods of data collection in qualitative research: Interviews and focus groups. *British Dental Journal, 204*(6), 291–295. https://doi.org/10.1038/bdj.2008.192

Hammersley, M., & Atkinson, P. (2019). *Ethnography: Principles in practice* (4th ed.). Routledge.

Harms, C., Brookhuis, K., & De Waard, D. (2015). Gamification of survey tools: Engaging participants through play. *Computers in Human Behavior, 51*, 255–261. https://doi.org/10.1016/j.chb.2015.05.054

Krueger, R. A., & Casey, M. A. (2015). *Focus groups: A practical guide for applied research* (5th ed.). SAGE Publications.

Markham, A., & Buchanan, E. (2012). Ethical decision-making and Internet research: Recommendations from the AoIR ethics working committee. Retrieved from https://aoir.org/reports/ethics2.pdf

Mavletova, A., & Couper, M. P. (2015). Mobile web survey design: Scrolling versus paging, SMS versus email invitations. *Journal of Survey Statistics and Methodology, 3*(4), 498–518. https://doi.org/10.1093/jssam/smv026

Morgan, D. L. (1997). *Focus groups as qualitative research* (2nd ed.). SAGE Publications.

Murthy, D. (2008). Digital ethnography: An examination of the use of new technologies for social research. *Sociology, 42*(5), 837–855. https://doi.org/10.1177/0038038508094565

O'Connor, H., Madge, C., Shaw, R., & Wellens, J. (2008). Internet-based interviewing. In N. Fielding, R. M. Lee, & G. Blank (Eds.), *The SAGE handbook of online research methods* (pp. 271–289). SAGE Publications.

Seitz, S. (2016). Pixilated partnerships, overcoming obstacles in qualitative interviews via Skype: A research note. *Qualitative Research, 16*(2), 229–235. https://doi.org/10.1177/1468794115577011

Silverman, D. (2020). *Qualitative research* (5th ed.). SAGE Publications.

Stewart, D. W., & Shamdasani, P. N. (2017). *Focus groups: Theory and practice* (3rd ed.). SAGE Publications.

Tuten, T. L., & Solomon, M. R. (2017). *Social media marketing* (3rd ed.). SAGE Publications.

Wright, K. B. (2005). Researching Internet-based populations: Advantages and disadvantages of online survey research, online questionnaire authoring software packages, and web survey services. *Journal of Computer-Mediated Communication, 10*(3). https://doi.org/10.1111/j.1083-6101.2005.tb00259.x

Chapter 05

Strategic Research Planning

5.1 Setting Objectives and Defining Research Questions.
5.2 Sampling Techniques: Purposive, Snowball, and Digital Sampling.
5.3 Designing Study Protocols for Digital and Hybrid Environments.
5.4 Addressing Bias in Strategic Research.

Strategic research planning is the backbone of any successful investigation, ensuring that studies are methodical, aligned with objectives, and capable of generating meaningful insights. This chapter delves into the intricacies of research planning, discussing how to set objectives and define research questions, choose appropriate sampling techniques, design protocols for digital and hybrid environments, and address potential biases.

5.1 Setting Objectives and Defining Research Questions

Importance of Research Objectives

Research objectives serve as the guiding principles for any study, outlining what the researcher aims to achieve. They are particularly crucial in strategic planning, as they help to focus efforts, allocate resources effectively, and measure outcomes (Creswell & Creswell, 2018). Objectives must be SMART: Specific, Measurable, Achievable, Relevant, and Time-bound.

For example, in a study on digital technology's role in ecotourism, an objective might be to evaluate the effectiveness of mobile apps in enhancing visitor engagement. By clearly defining such objectives, researchers can align their methodologies and analyses to address specific goals.

Formulating Research Questions

Research questions are derived from the objectives and are the foundation of the study. They should be clear, concise, and exploratory in nature, particularly in qualitative research. Well-framed questions address the "what," "how," or "why" of the research topic, helping to guide data collection and analysis (Bryman, 2016).

In the context of strategic research planning, questions might include:

- What are the key challenges in integrating digital tools into ecotourism practices?
- How can hybrid research methodologies enhance data collection in ecotourism studies?

These questions determine the scope and depth of the investigation, ensuring that the research remains relevant and targeted.

5.2 Sampling Techniques: Purposive, Snowball, and Digital Sampling

Purposive Sampling

Purposive sampling, also known as judgemental sampling, involves selecting participants based on specific characteristics relevant to the research objectives. This method ensures that the sample is information-rich and capable of providing valuable insights (Patton, 2015). For instance, in a study on ecotourism, researchers might select stakeholders such as park managers, tour operators, and local community leaders to gather diverse perspectives.

Advantages of purposive sampling include its flexibility and ability to focus on key informants. However, it may introduce selection bias if not applied rigorously (Etikan et al. 2016).

Snowball Sampling

Snowball sampling is particularly useful for accessing hard-to-reach populations, such as niche tourism stakeholders or marginalised communities. This technique involves initial participants referring others, creating a chain of referrals (Biernacki & Waldorf, 1981). While this method is efficient for building trust and accessing networks, it can lead to sample homogeneity if participants share similar characteristics.

Digital Sampling

The rise of digital platforms has transformed sampling techniques, enabling researchers to reach diverse populations efficiently. Online communities, social media platforms, and digital forums offer rich sources for participant recruitment (Baltar & Brunet, 2012). For example, researchers studying ecotourism can engage with online travel communities or social media groups focused on sustainable travel.

Digital sampling is cost-effective and scalable but requires careful consideration of ethical issues, such as participant consent and data privacy (Markham & Buchanan, 2012).

5.3 Designing Study Protocols for Digital and Hybrid Environments

Digital Study Protocols

Digital environments demand tailored protocols that leverage technology to facilitate data collection and analysis. Protocols should address the use of tools such as online surveys, video conferencing for interviews, and digital ethnography for observational studies (Hewson et al., 2016).

Key considerations in designing digital protocols include:

- **Tool Selection**: Choosing user-friendly platforms like Zoom, Qualtrics, or NVivo to ensure seamless data collection.
- **Participant Engagement**: Employing strategies such as gamification or interactive elements to maintain participant interest.
- **Data Security**: Ensuring robust measures to protect participant data, such as encryption and secure storage.

Hybrid Study Protocols

Hybrid approaches combine traditional and digital methods, offering the flexibility to adapt to participants' preferences. For example, researchers can conduct in-person focus groups supplemented by online surveys to maximise data richness and reach (Stewart & Shamdasani, 2017).

Hybrid protocols must address logistical challenges, such as synchronising data from multiple sources and ensuring consistency in participant experiences. They also require careful planning to manage resources effectively, particularly when transitioning between physical and digital settings (Flick, 2018).

5.4 Addressing Bias in Strategic Research

Types of Bias

Bias in research can manifest in various forms, including selection bias, confirmation bias, and procedural bias. Addressing these biases is critical to ensuring the validity and reliability of findings (Robson & McCartan, 2016).

- **Selection Bias**: Occurs when the sample does not adequately represent the population. Techniques such as stratified sampling or random selection can mitigate this issue.
- **Confirmation Bias**: Arises when researchers unconsciously seek data that supports their hypotheses. Employing triangulation and peer debriefing can help counteract this bias.
- **Procedural Bias**: Results from inconsistencies in data collection processes. Standardised protocols and training for researchers can reduce procedural bias.

Strategies for Mitigating Bias

1. **Triangulation**: Combining multiple data sources, methods, or theoretical perspectives to cross-verify findings (Denzin, 2017). For example, integrating interviews, surveys, and observational data ensures a holistic understanding of the research topic.

2. **Reflexivity**: Researchers should critically reflect on their assumptions, positionality, and potential influence on the research process (Berger, 2015). Maintaining a reflexive journal can help document these reflections.
3. **Participant Validation**: Involving participants in validating findings ensures that interpretations accurately reflect their perspectives, reducing the risk of misrepresentation.

Conclusion

Strategic research planning requires meticulous attention to setting objectives, defining research questions, selecting appropriate sampling techniques, and designing robust protocols for both digital and hybrid environments. Addressing potential biases through strategies like triangulation and reflexivity further enhances the credibility and validity of the research. By embracing innovative methodologies and adhering to rigorous standards, researchers can ensure that their studies generate meaningful, actionable insights, particularly in dynamic fields like digital technology and ecotourism.

References

Baltar, F., & Brunet, I. (2012). Social research 2.0: Virtual snowball sampling method using Facebook. *Internet Research, 22*(1), 57–74. https://doi.org/10.1108/10662241211199960

Berger, R. (2015). Now I see it, now I don't: Researcher's position and reflexivity in qualitative research. *Qualitative Research, 15*(2), 219–234. https://doi.org/10.1177/1468794112468475

Biernacki, P., & Waldorf, D. (1981). Snowball sampling: Problems and techniques of chain referral sampling. *Sociological Methods & Research, 10*(2), 141–163. https://doi.org/10.1177/004912418101000205

Bryman, A. (2016). *Social research methods* (5th ed.). Oxford University Press.

Creswell, J. W., & Creswell, J. D. (2018). *Research design: Qualitative, quantitative, and mixed methods approaches* (5th ed.). SAGE Publications.

Denzin, N. K. (2017). *The research act: A theoretical introduction to sociological methods* (4th ed.). Routledge.

Etikan, I., Musa, S. A., & Alkassim, R. S. (2016). Comparison of convenience sampling and purposive sampling. *American Journal of Theoretical and Applied Statistics, 5*(1), 1–4. https://doi.org/10.11648/j.ajtas.20160501.11

Flick, U. (2018). *An introduction to qualitative research* (6th ed.). SAGE Publications.

Hewson, C., Vogel, C., & Laurent, D. (2016). *Internet research methods* (2nd ed.). SAGE Publications.

Markham, A., & Buchanan, E. (2012). Ethical decision-making and Internet research: Recommendations from the AoIR ethics working committee. Retrieved from https://aoir.org/reports/ethics2.pdf

Patton, M. Q. (2015). *Qualitative research and evaluation methods* (4th ed.). SAGE Publications.

Robson, C., & McCartan, K. (2016). *Real world research* (4th ed.). Wiley.

Stewart, D. W., & Shamdasani, P. N. (2017). *Focus groups: Theory and practice* (3rd ed.). SAGE Publications.

Chapter 06

Analysing Qualitative Data

6.1 Coding and Thematic Analysis.
6.2 Digital Tools for Analysis: NVivo, ATLAS.ti, and AI-driven Platforms.
6.3 Content Analysis vs. Discourse Analysis.
6.4 Visualising Qualitative Insights.
6.5 PRISMA Checklist

Qualitative data analysis involves systematically examining and interpreting non-numeric information to uncover patterns, themes, and insights. As research increasingly embraces digital tools, the analysis process has evolved, becoming more robust and efficient. This chapter explores key techniques for analysing qualitative data, including coding and thematic analysis, the use of digital tools, comparisons between content and discourse analysis, and methods for visualising qualitative insights.

6.1 Coding and Thematic Analysis

The Role of Coding in Qualitative Analysis

Coding is the foundational process in qualitative data analysis, enabling researchers to categorise data into meaningful units. It involves assigning labels or codes to specific segments of text, images, or other data forms based on their relevance to the research questions (Saldaña, 2021). For instance, in a study on digital technology in ecotourism, codes might include "digital tools," "sustainability," and "community involvement."

Types of Coding

- **Open Coding**: Initial identification of concepts without predetermined categories (Strauss & Corbin, 1998).
- **Axial Coding**: Organising open codes into broader themes by identifying relationships between them.
- **Selective Coding**: Refining and integrating codes to form a coherent narrative or theory.

Thematic Analysis

Thematic analysis involves identifying, analysing, and reporting patterns or themes within data. It is a flexible method applicable to diverse research paradigms (Braun & Clarke, 2006, 2017). The process typically includes:

a. Familiarisation with data: Repeated reading or observation to immerse oneself in the data.
b. Generating initial codes: Systematically coding significant features of the data.
c. Searching for themes: Grouping codes into overarching themes.
d. Reviewing themes: Ensuring themes are internally coherent and consistent with the data.
e. Defining and naming themes: Creating clear definitions and labels for each theme.
f. Producing the report: The final opportunity for analysis. Selection of vivid, compelling extract examples, final analysis of selected extracts, relating back of the analysis to the research question and literature, producing a scholarly report of the analysis. Thematic analysis is particularly valuable in uncovering hidden meanings and exploring complex social phenomena, such as the interplay between technology and sustainable tourism.

Table 1. A 15-Point Checklist of Criteria for Good Thematic Analysis

Process (Stages)	Point	Criteria (Application)
Transcription	1	Data has been transcribed to the appropriate level of detail and checked against digital audio tapes for accuracy in case of doubt.
Coding	2	Each data item has been given equal attention in the coding process, which was demonstrated on Microsoft Excel in the form of a data grid.
	3	Themes emerged in this study have been generated from a thorough coding process and are inclusive and comprehensive.
	4	Relevant extracts generated in this study for each theme have been combined or collated using a data grid.
	5	Themes emerged from each construct have been checked thoroughly and confirmed with the original data.
	6	Themes are internally logical, consistent with distinctive features.

Analysis	7	The data analysis process was very thorough, explained, and provided relevant answers to the research questions.
	8	The findings from the original data match each other based on the interview extracts.
	9	The data analysis provides convincing and well-organised findings from the data which reflect the main aims of the research.
	10	This study produces a good balance between analytic narrative using quotes from the data extracts and tables/figures where necessary.
Overall	11	The researcher devoted enough time to complete all the six phases (stages) of the thematic analysis without rushing a single phase.
Written report	12	The process of analysis, assumptions, and a specific approach to thematic analysis are well explained to the readers of this thesis.
	13	The method reported to analyse this study was thematic analysis, and it was actually used. Therefore, the reported analyses are consistent.
	14	Interpretative paradigm was adopted in this study; therefore, the language and concepts used in writing the findings are consistent with the epistemological position of the analysis and presentation.
	15	The researcher is positioned as being in and with the study context to elicit detailed information from the selected respondents. Therefore, themes do not just 'cmerge' but are brought up through the sharing of experiences by the participants in this study.

Source: Adapted from (Braun & Clarke, 2006, 2017).

6.2 Digital Tools for Analysis: NVivo, ATLAS.ti, and AI-driven Platforms

NVivo

NVivo is a widely used qualitative data analysis software that facilitates coding, theme development, and data visualisation. Its features include:

- Importing and analysing text, audio, video, and social media data.
- Auto-coding capabilities for faster processing.
- Visualisation tools such as word clouds and cluster maps (Edhlund & McDougall, 2019).

For example, NVivo can be used to analyse interview transcripts from stakeholders in sustainable forest management, highlighting recurring themes like "community empowerment" or "digital innovation."

ATLAS.ti

ATLAS.ti is another popular tool that supports qualitative and mixed methods research. It offers:

- A user-friendly interface for coding and memo-writing.
- Network-building features to visualise relationships between codes and themes.
- Compatibility with large datasets, making it ideal for complex studies (Friese, 2019).

AI-Driven Platforms

AI-driven tools like Dedoose and thematic.ai have revolutionised qualitative analysis by automating coding processes and identifying patterns using machine learning algorithms (Xu & Wang, 2022). While these tools enhance efficiency, researchers must critically assess AI-generated insights to ensure validity and context relevance.

Advantages and Challenges of Digital Tools

Digital tools streamline analysis, enabling researchers to handle larger datasets and generate visual outputs. However, they require technical proficiency, and reliance on automation may overlook nuanced insights (Silver & Lewins, 2014).

6.3 Content Analysis vs. Discourse Analysis

[a]. Content Analysis.

Content analysis is a systematic method for quantifying and analysing textual data. It focuses on identifying the frequency and context of specific words, phrases, or concepts (Krippendorff, 2018). For example, analysing online reviews of ecotourism apps could reveal recurring concerns about usability or sustainability impact.

Key Steps:

1. **Defining categories**: Establishing clear coding categories based on research objectives.
2. **Coding**: Assigning data to categories.
3. **Interpreting results**: Analysing patterns and drawing conclusions.

Content analysis is particularly effective for summarising large datasets and generating actionable insights.

[2]. Discourse Analysis

Discourse analysis examines how language is used to construct meaning within specific social, cultural, or political contexts (Fairclough, 2013). Unlike content analysis, it delves deeper into the underlying ideologies, power dynamics, and assumptions embedded in the text.

For instance, discourse analysis could explore how ecotourism marketing materials frame narratives of "authenticity" or "sustainability," revealing their impact on consumer perceptions.

Comparison

While content analysis emphasises frequency and patterns, discourse analysis focuses on interpretation and context. Both methods are valuable, and their applicability depends on the research goals. Combining the two can provide a comprehensive understanding of textual data.

6.4 Visualising Qualitative Insights

Importance of Visualisation

Visualising qualitative data enhances comprehension and communication of findings. It translates complex themes into intuitive formats, making results accessible to diverse audiences (Miles et al., 2020).

Common Visualisation Techniques

1. **Word Clouds**: Highlight frequently occurring terms in a dataset, offering a quick overview of dominant themes.
2. **Concept Maps**: Depict relationships between themes and sub-themes, aiding in the exploration of complex ideas.
3. **Timelines**: Visualise sequences of events or processes, such as the adoption of digital tools in ecotourism.
4. **Heat Maps**: Represent data density or intensity, useful for geospatial analyses in studies involving GIS tools.

Software for Visualisation

- **NVivo and ATLAS.ti**: Offer integrated visualisation tools.
- **Tableau and Power BI**: Facilitate advanced visualisations, particularly for presenting mixed methods data.
- **Dedoose**: Combines visualisation with coding capabilities for streamlined analysis.

Challenges in Visualisation

Effective visualisation requires careful planning to avoid oversimplification or misrepresentation of data. Researchers must balance aesthetic appeal with accuracy and context (Tufte, 2006).

6.5 PRISMA Checklists

PRISMA Checklists PRISMA checklists has been in existence for medical research under a different name called Quality of Reporting of Meta-analyses (QUOROM) Statement since 1996. It was developed to address the suboptimal reporting of meta-analyses (Moher, et al., 2009). This was renamed as Preferred Reporting Items for Systematic Reviews and Meta-Analyses (PRISMA) in 2009. The main reason for replacing the initial name from QUOROM to PRISMA was the need to include both systematic and meta-analyses (Moher, et al., 2009). Based on this update, definitions for systematic reviews and meta-analyses were adopted from the work of Green and Higgins (2005). For example, a systematic review is a review of a clearly formulated question that uses systematic and explicit methods to identify, select, and critically appraise relevant research, and to collect and analyse data from the studies that are included in the review. On the other hand, meta-analysis refers to the use of statistical techniques in a systematic review to integrate the results of included studies (Green & Higgins, 2005).

PRISMA is a protocol developed to conduct systematic reviews consisting of a four-phase or stage flow diagram (refer to Figure 1), and a 27-item checklist (refer to Table 1). These checklists were developed in the medical field by a group of 29 scholars including review authors, methodologists, clinicians, medical editors and a consumer. PRISMA was adopted at a three-day meeting held in Ottawa, Canada, in June 2005 (Moher et al., 2009). The choice of PRISMA over other protocols is due to the recognition of its comprehensiveness, its applications in several academic disciplines across the world beyond the medical fields, and PRISMA potential to increase consistency of literature reviews among the researchers (Liberati et al., 2009). In addition, the adoption of PRISMA is aimed at instilling accuracy and transparency of academic literature review. The current study focuses on the PRISMA checklists protocol and to highlight the paucity of its application in hospitality and tourism research.

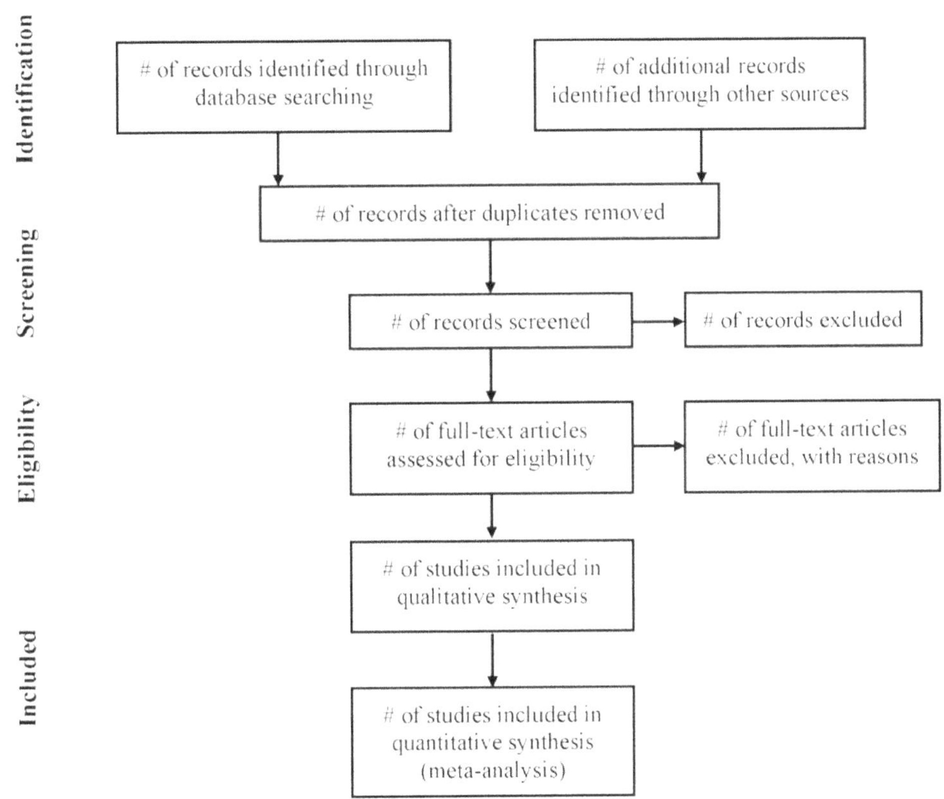

Figure 1. The PRISMA flow diagram.

Source: *Adapted from Moher et al. (2009); Pati and Lorusso (2018); Pahlevan-Sharif et al. (2019).*

Table 2. PRISMA checklist of items: Synopsis for research

Section/Topic	Number	PRISMA checklist item
TITLE		
Title	1	Identify the report as a systematic review, meta-analysis or both.
ABSTRACT		
Structured summary	2	Provide a structured summary including, as applicable; objectives; data sources; study eligibility criteria, participants, and interventions.
INTRODUCTION		
Rationale	3	Describe the rational for the review in the context of what is already known
Objectives	4	Provide an explicit statement of questions being addressed with reference to participants, interventions, comparisons, outcomes, and study design (PICOS).

METHODS		
Protocol and registration	5	Indicate if a review protocol exists, if and where it can be accessed
Eligibility	6	Specify study characteristics (e.g., PICOS, length of follow-up) and report characteristics (e.g., years considered, language, publication status) used as criteria for eligibility, giving rationale.
Information sources	7	Describe all information sources (e.g., databases with dates of coverage, contact with study authors to identify additional studies) in the search and date last searched.
Search	8	Present full electronic search strategy for at least one database, including any limits used, such that it could be repeated.
Study selection	9	State the process for selecting studies (i.e., screening, eligibility, included in systematic review, and, if applicable, included in the meta-analysis).
Data collection process	10	Describe method of data extraction from reports (e.g., piloted forms, independently, in duplicate) and any processes for obtaining and confirming data from investigators.
Data items	11	List and define all variables for which data were sought (e.g., PICOS, funding sources) and any assumptions and simplifications made.
Risk of bias in Individual studies	12	Describe methods used for assessing risk of bias of individual studies (including specification of whether this was done at the study or outcome level), and how this information is to be used in any data synthesis.
Summary measures	13	State the principal summary measures e.g. risk ratio, difference in means.
Synthesis of results	14	Describe the methods of handling data and combining results of studies, if done, including measures of consistency (e.g. I2) for each meta-analysis.
Risk of bias across	15	Specify any assessment of risk of bias that may affect the cumulative evidence (e.g., publication bias, selective reporting within studies).
Additional analyses	16	Describe methods of additional analyses (e.g., sensitivity or subgroup analyses, meta-regression), if done, indicating which were pre-specified.

Study selection a flow diagram.	17	Give numbers of studies screened, assessed for eligibility, and included in the review, with reasons for exclusions at each stage, ideally with
Study characteristics	18	For each study, present characteristics for which data were extract extracted (e.g., study size, PICOS, follow-up period) and provide the citations.
Risk of bias with studies	19	Present data on risk of bias of each study and, if available, any outcome-level assessment (see Item 12).
Results of individual Studies	20	For all outcomes considered (benefits or harms), present, for each study: (a) simple summary data for each intervention group and (b) effect estimates and confidence intervals, ideally with a forest plot.
Synthesis of results	21	Present results of each meta-analysis done, including confidence intervals and measures of consistency.
Risk of bias across studies	22	Present results of any assessment of risk of bias across studies (see item 15).
Additional analysis	23	Give results of additional analyses, if done (e.g., sensitivity or subgroup analyses, meta-regression [see Item 16]).
DISCUSSION		
Summary of evidence	24	Summarize the main findings including the strength of evidence for each main outcome; consider their relevance to key groups (e.g., health care providers, users, and policy makers).
Limitations	25	Discuss limitations at study and outcome level (e.g., risk of bias), and at review level (e.g., incomplete retrieval of identified research, reporting bias).
Conclusions	26	Provide a general interpretation of the results in the context of other evidence, and implications for future research.
FUNDING	27	Describe sources of funding for the systematic review and other support (e.g., supply of data); role of funders for the systematic review.

Source: *Adopted from Moher, et al. (2009); Pati and Lorusso (2018); Pahlevan-Sharif et al. (2019).*

Conclusion

Analysing qualitative data is a multifaceted process requiring meticulous coding, thoughtful use of digital tools, and a clear understanding of different analytical approaches. Techniques like thematic analysis, supported by tools such as NVivo and ATLAS.ti, enable researchers to uncover patterns and generate actionable insights. Comparing methods like content and discourse analysis further enriches the research process, offering both depth and breadth. Visualisation plays a crucial role in communicating findings effectively, ensuring that complex qualitative insights are accessible and impactful. Moreover, the PRISMA framework is also an important data collection and analysis technique in both social science and medical research. By adopting these advanced methodologies and leveraging technological innovations, researchers can navigate the complexities of qualitative analysis and contribute meaningful knowledge to their respective fields.

References

Braun, V., & Clarke, V. (2006). Using thematic analysis in psychology. *Qualitative Research in Psychology, 3*(2), 77–101. https://doi.org/10.1191/1478088706qp063oa

Braun, V., & Clarke, V. (2017). Thematic analysis. The Journal of Positive Psychology, 12 (3), 297–298. https://doi.org/10.1080/17439760.1262613

Edhlund, B., & McDougall, A. (2019). *NVivo 12 essentials*. Lulu Press.

Fairclough, N. (2013). *Critical discourse analysis: The critical study of language* (2nd ed.). Routledge.

Friese, S. (2019). *ATLAS.ti 8 user manual*. ATLAS.ti.

Green S, Higgins J, (editors) (2005). Glossary. *Cochrane handbook for systematic reviews of interventions 4.2.5. The Cochrane Collaboration*. https://training.cochrane.org/handbook#how-to-access

Krippendorff, K. (2018). *Content analysis: An introduction to its methodology* (4th ed.). SAGE Publications.

Liberati, A., Altman, D., Tetzlaff, J., Mulrow, C., Gøtzsche, P., Ioannidis, J.,... Moher, D. (2009). The PRISMA statement for reporting systematic reviews and meta-analyses of studies that evaluate healthcare interventions: Explanation and elaboration. *PLoS Medicine, 6*(7), e1000100.

Miles, M. B., Huberman, A. M., & Saldaña, J. (2020). *Qualitative data analysis: A methods sourcebook* (4th ed.). SAGE Publications.

Moher, D., Liberati, A., Tetzlaff, J. Altman. D.G., The PRISMA Group. (2009). Preferred Reporting Items for Systematic Reviews and Meta-Analyses: The PRISMA Statement. PLoS Med 6(7): e1000097. doi:10.1371/journal.pmed.1000097

Pahlevan-Sharif, S., Mura, P., & Wijesinghe, S. N. R. (2019). A systematic review of systematic reviews in tourism. Journal of Hospitality & Tourism Management, 39, 158-165. https://doi.org/10.1016/j.jhtm.2019.04.001

Pati, D., & Lorusso, L. N. (2017). How to write a systematic review of the literature. Health EnvironmentsResearch&DesignJournals,11(1),15-30.DOI:10.1177/1937586717747384

Saldaña, J. (2021). *The coding manual for qualitative researchers* (4th ed.). SAGE Publications.

Silver, C., & Lewins, A. (2014). *Using software in qualitative research: A step-by-step guide.* SAGE Publications.

Strauss, A., & Corbin, J. (1998). *Basics of qualitative research: Techniques and procedures for developing grounded theory* (2nd ed.). SAGE Publications.

Tufte, E. R. (2006). *The visual display of quantitative information* (2nd ed.). Graphics Press.

Xu, L., & Wang, J. (2022). Exploring the role of artificial intelligence in qualitative data analysis: Potentials and pitfalls. *Journal of Mixed Methods Research, 16*(3), 374–391. https://doi.org/10.1177/15586898211064832

6.6 Thematic.ai: Revolutionising Qualitative Data Analysis

Introduction to Thematic.ai

Thematic.ai is an AI-powered qualitative data analysis platform designed to simplify and enhance the process of identifying themes, patterns, and insights from text-based data. It leverages machine learning (ML) algorithms and natural language processing (NLP) to automate key stages of qualitative analysis, offering researchers, businesses, and organisations an efficient tool for handling large datasets, such as survey responses, customer feedback, and interview transcripts.

Thematic.ai is particularly valuable for researchers dealing with vast amounts of unstructured data. It reduces manual effort, ensures consistency, and accelerates the discovery of actionable insights (Thematic, 2023).

Key Features of Thematic.ai

Automated Theme Detection

Thematic.ai uses AI algorithms to automatically identify recurring themes in textual data. This feature eliminates the need for researchers to manually code large datasets, significantly reducing time and effort while maintaining consistency. For example, in a study on digital ecotourism, Thematic.ai can analyse visitor reviews to identify common themes like "app usability," "sustainability impact," and "visitor satisfaction."

Customisation and Refinement

While the platform automates initial theme detection, users retain control over the process. Researchers can refine themes, merge similar categories, or adjust the analysis based on their contextual understanding of the data (Ghahramani et al., 2021).

Real-Time Analysis

Thematic.ai enables real-time analysis, making it ideal for organisations that need to process incoming data quickly. This feature is especially useful in business settings, such as monitoring customer sentiment from ongoing feedback (Thematic, 2023).

Interactive Dashboards

The platform includes interactive visualisations like heat maps, word clouds, and trend graphs. These tools allow users to explore data intuitively and communicate findings effectively.

Integration Capabilities

Thematic.ai integrates seamlessly with platforms like SurveyMonkey, Zendesk, and Slack, enabling direct import of data for analysis (Smith et al., 2022).

Applications of Thematic.ai

Academic Research

Researchers can use Thematic.ai to analyse qualitative data such as open-ended survey responses, interview transcripts, and focus group discussions. The platform is especially helpful in large-scale studies where manual coding would be impractical.

Business Analytics

Organisations leverage Thematic.ai to extract insights from customer feedback, product reviews, and employee surveys, helping them identify areas for improvement and track sentiment trends over time (Ghahramani et al., 2021).

Policy Analysis

Policymakers can use Thematic.ai to assess public opinion from consultation documents or social media data, identifying key themes and concerns efficiently.

Advantages of Thematic.ai

Efficiency and Scalability.

Thematic.ai can analyse vast amounts of data in a fraction of the time it would take to do manually. This scalability makes it a valuable tool for projects with extensive datasets.

Consistency in Coding.

AI algorithms minimise subjective bias in theme identification, ensuring a consistent approach to data analysis.

Enhanced Insights

Thematic.ai uncovers hidden patterns and trends that might be overlooked in manual analysis, enhancing the depth and quality of insights (Smith et al., 2022).

Challenges and Limitations

Reliance on Algorithms

While Thematic.ai is powerful, it relies on algorithms that may not fully capture the nuances of qualitative data. Researchers must critically evaluate AI-generated themes to ensure contextual accuracy (Ghahramani et al. 2021).

Learning Curve

Although user-friendly, the platform requires initial training to maximise its potential, especially for researchers unfamiliar with AI-driven tools.

Cost Implications

Thematic.ai is a premium service, which may not be accessible to all researchers or organisations.

Thematic.ai in the Context of Digital Ecotourism Research

In studies related to digital technology and sustainable forest management for promoting ecotourism, Thematic.ai offers significant potential. By analysing visitor feedback or stakeholder interviews, it can identify recurring themes such as digital adoption barriers, user experiences, and perceptions of sustainability initiatives. This data can guide strategic decision-making, improve policy frameworks, and enhance user engagement in ecotourism practices.

For instance, a thematic analysis using Thematic.ai might reveal that visitors value "real-time navigation features" in ecotourism apps but are concerned about "limited offline functionality," highlighting areas for improvement.

Conclusion

Thematic.ai represents a significant advancement in qualitative data analysis, enabling researchers to handle large datasets efficiently while uncovering actionable insights. Its automated theme detection, user-friendly interface, and interactive visualisations make it a valuable tool across academia, business, and policy settings. However, it is essential to complement its capabilities with human expertise to ensure accurate and contextually relevant interpretations.

References

Ghahramani, Z., Rahimi, R., & Kopec, D. (2021). Exploring the role of AI in qualitative research: Potentials and challenges. *International Journal of Social Research Methodology, 24*(3), 315–329. https://doi.org/10.1080/13645579.2021.1873407

Smith, J. T., Williams, L., & Chen, R. (2022). Advancing customer feedback analysis through AI-driven platforms: A case study on Thematic.ai. *Journal of Business Research, 139*, 548–556. https://doi.org/10.1016/j.jbusres.2021.10.001

Thematic. (2023). Transforming qualitative research with AI-driven insights. Retrieved from https://www.thematic.ai

SECTION III

Advanced Topics in Qualitative Research

Chapter 07

Digital Ethnography

7.1 Conducting Ethnography in Online Communities.
7.2 Netnography: Researching Social Media Spaces.
7.3 Ethical Dilemmas in Digital Ethnography.

Digital ethnography is a contemporary methodological approach in qualitative research that focuses on studying cultures, behaviours, and interactions in digital and online environments. This chapter delves into three core aspects: conducting ethnography in online communities, netnography as a technique for exploring Social Media Spaces, and addressing ethical dilemmas inherent in digital ethnographic research.

7.1 Conducting Ethnography in Online Communities

Defining Digital Ethnography

Ethnography traditionally involves immersive fieldwork to understand cultural practices, beliefs, and social interactions (Hine, 2015). In digital ethnography, the "field" shifts to online spaces such as forums, chatrooms, blogs, and virtual worlds. This method allows researchers to study communities and interactions that exist exclusively or primarily in digital environments.

Methodological Framework

Conducting digital ethnography requires adaptation to the unique characteristics of online spaces. Researchers often rely on participant observation, in-depth interviews, and digital artefacts, such as screenshots or archived conversations, as data sources. Key steps include:

- **Defining the Field**: Identifying the digital community to study, such as a subreddit or an MMORPG (Boellstorff et al., 2012).
- **Gaining Access**: Joining communities, gaining trust, and ensuring transparency in research intentions.
- **Documenting Interactions**: Recording conversations, capturing digital behaviours, and analysing multimedia content.
- **Reflexivity**: Acknowledging the researcher's positionality and its impact on the interpretation of data (Markham, 2017).

Applications in Research

Digital ethnography has been instrumental in fields like marketing, where researchers analyse consumer behaviours, and sociology, where studies focus on online activism or digital subcultures. For instance, examining how users in a climate change forum share resources provides insights into collaborative knowledge-sharing practices (Hine, 2015).

7.2 Netnography: Researching Social Media Spaces

Origins and Definition

Coined by Kozinets (2015), netnography is a specialised form of digital ethnography tailored to studying social media platforms. It focuses on understanding user-generated content, interactions, and the cultural significance of social media activities.

Key Features of Netnography

Immersion in Online Platforms: Netnographers engage with platforms like Instagram, Twitter, or TikTok to observe trends, hashtags, and user communities.

Adaptation of Traditional Methods: While retaining ethnography's core principles, netnography incorporates digital techniques like analysing hashtags and algorithms (Kozinets, 2020).

Rapid Data Collection: Social media platforms generate vast amounts of real-time data, enabling researchers to capture dynamic cultural shifts.

Techniques in Netnography

- **Data Mining**: Extracting posts, comments, and interactions from social media using tools like NVivo or MAXQDA.
- **Sentiment Analysis**: Employing NLP to gauge the emotional tone of posts and comments.
- **Visual Analysis**: Studying memes, emojis, and video content to interpret cultural expressions (Marres, 2017).

Case Study Applications

Netnography has been used to understand topics like brand loyalty, political activism, and health communication. For example, a study on Instagram hashtags related to sustainable living can reveal public attitudes towards environmental consciousness (Kozinets, 2020).

7.3 Ethical Dilemmas in Digital Ethnography

Privacy Concerns

Unlike traditional ethnography, where consent is often explicit, digital ethnography must navigate ambiguous notions of privacy in online spaces. Researchers face ethical dilemmas in determining whether online interactions are public or private, particularly on platforms with unclear boundaries (Markham & Buchanan, 2017).

Informed Consent

Informed consent is challenging in digital ethnography, as researchers may encounter large groups where obtaining individual consent is impractical. Strategies include providing disclosures in community posts or focusing on public data (Bruckman, 2014).

Anonymity and Data Security

Ensuring anonymity is critical to protecting participants from harm. Researchers often anonymise usernames and redact identifying details. However, storing digital data securely remains a significant challenge, requiring robust encryption and access controls (Hine, 2015).

Balancing Observation and Participation

Digital ethnographers often grapple with their role as participant-observers. Active participation may influence the community, raising questions about authenticity and objectivity (Markham, 2017).

Ethical Case Study

A study on online grief communities revealed ethical dilemmas when participants shared personal experiences of loss. Researchers had to navigate how to document these interactions respectfully while avoiding exploitation of sensitive narratives (Bruckman, 2014).

Conclusion

Digital ethnography, including its specialised form netnography, represents an evolution in qualitative research methodologies, addressing the complexities of studying online spaces. It offers unparalleled access to rich, unstructured data from digital communities and social media platforms, making it invaluable for contemporary cultural and social research. However, ethical considerations, including privacy, consent, and data security, remain paramount to its application. Future advancements in digital ethnography may include AI-powered tools for deeper insights and augmented reality (AR) environments, further expanding the boundaries of qualitative research.

References

Boellstorff, T., Nardi, B., Pearce, C., & Taylor, T. L. (2012). *Ethnography and virtual worlds: A handbook of method.* Princeton University Press. https://doi.org/10.1515/9781400845286

Bruckman, A. (2014). Research ethics and HCI. *Ways of knowing in HCI,* 449-468. Springer.

Hine, C. (2015). *Ethnography for the Internet: Embedded, embodied and everyday.* Bloomsbury.

Kozinets, R. V. (2015). *Netnography: Redefined.* SAGE Publications.

Kozinets, R. V. (2020). Social media analytics: merging big data and qualitative insights. *Journal of Marketing Theory and Practice, 28*(1), 152-166. https://doi.org/10.1080/10696679.2019.1704423

Markham, A. (2017). The methods, politics, and ethics of representation in online ethnography. *The SAGE handbook of qualitative research,* 650-668.

Markham, A., & Buchanan, E. (2017). Ethical considerations in digital research contexts. *Research Ethics in the Digital Age,* 119-135.

Marres, N. (2017). *Digital sociology: The reinvention of social research.* Polity Press.

Chapter 08

Case Study Methodology

8.1 Designing a Qualitative Case Study.
8.2 Integrating Digital Evidence in Case Studies.
8.3 Strategic Case Analysis for Policy and Practice.

The **case study methodology** is a vital research approach, particularly in qualitative studies, as it offers in-depth insights into specific phenomena within real-life contexts (Yin, 2018). This chapter focuses on the design of qualitative case studies, the integration of digital evidence, and strategic case analysis for policy and practice.

8.1 Designing a Qualitative Case Study

The design of a Qualitative Case Study involves identifying a research problem that benefits from contextual understanding. This section emphasises five key components:

- **Defining the Case**: The case must be clearly bounded, focusing on a person, group, organisation, event, or issue (Creswell & Poth, 2017).
- **Setting the Research Objectives**: Objectives should align with the research questions, ensuring the case study is purposeful (Stake, 1995).
- **Case Selection**: Researchers employ strategies such as purposive sampling to ensure the case is relevant and representative. Multiple case designs may also be used for comparative analysis (Yin, 2018).
- **Data Collection Methods**: Methods include interviews, observations, documents, and multimedia sources. Triangulation ensures the validity and reliability of the findings (Flick, 2018).
- **Data Analysis Framework**: Data is analysed using thematic analysis, grounded theory, or narrative analysis, depending on the study's focus (Miles, Huberman, & Saldana, 2014).

Ethical considerations are integral, including obtaining informed consent, ensuring confidentiality, and minimising potential biases (Creswell & Poth, 2017).

8.2 Integrating Digital Evidence in Case Studies

With technological advancements, the use of digital evidence has become crucial in case studies. This section explores how digital tools and data sources enhance the depth and accuracy of qualitative research.

- **Digital Data Sources:** Social media, online forums, blogs, emails, and organisational databases serve as rich sources of digital evidence (Bryman, 2021).
- **Analytical Tools:** Software like NVivo and MAXQDA supports the analysis of digital data, enabling the identification of patterns and themes (Silver & Lewins, 2014).
- **Ethical Challenges:** Issues like privacy, consent, and data security are heightened when using digital evidence. Researchers must adhere to ethical standards like anonymising data and complying with data protection laws (BPS, 2021).
- **Case Example:** A study investigating online consumer behaviour might analyse social media interactions and e-commerce data, showcasing how digital evidence reveals patterns otherwise inaccessible.

Integrating digital evidence facilitates a multidimensional understanding of the case, bridging traditional and modern research methods (Tracy, 2020).

8.3 Strategic Case Analysis for Policy and Practice

Strategic case analysis involves applying case study findings to inform policies and practices. This section outlines frameworks for translating research outcomes into actionable insights.

- **Frameworks for Strategic Analysis:**

SWOT Analysis: Examining strengths, weaknesses, opportunities, and threats provides a structured approach for understanding a case's implications.

Stakeholder Mapping: Identifying key stakeholders and their interests ensures that recommendations are practical and inclusive (Freeman, 1984).

- **Evidence-Based Policy Recommendations:** Findings from case studies guide decision-making by providing context-specific evidence (Nutley, Walter, & Davies, 2007).
- **Cross-Contextual Relevance:** While grounded in specific contexts, case study insights can be adapted to similar settings, enhancing their utility (Yin, 2018).

For example, a case study on community health interventions could inform policies aimed at addressing healthcare disparities, showcasing the method's practical relevance (Greenhalgh et al. 2018).

Conclusion

The case study methodology remains a powerful tool in qualitative research. Designing a robust study requires careful planning, while integrating digital evidence broadens analytical capabilities. Strategic analysis ensures that case studies contribute meaningfully to policy and practice, emphasising their transformative potential.

References

Bryman, A. (2021). *Social research methods* (6th ed.). Oxford University Press.

Creswell, J. W., & Poth, C. N. (2017). *Qualitative inquiry and research design: Choosing among five approaches* (4th ed.). SAGE Publications.

Flick, U. (2018). *An introduction to qualitative research* (6th ed.). SAGE Publications.

Freeman, R. E. (1984). *Strategic management: A stakeholder approach*. Cambridge University Press.

Greenhalgh, T., Robert, G., Bate, P., Macfarlane, F., & Kyriakidou, O. (2018). *Diffusion of innovations in health service organisations: A systematic literature review*. Wiley.

Miles, M. B., Huberman, A. M., & Saldana, J. (2014). *Qualitative data analysis: A methods sourcebook* (3rd ed.). SAGE Publications.

Nutley, S., Walter, I., & Davies, H. T. O. (2007). *Using evidence: How research can inform public services*. Policy Press.

Silver, C., & Lewins, A. (2014). *Using software in qualitative research: A step-by-step guide* (2nd ed.). SAGE Publications.

Stake, R. E. (1995). *The art of case study research*. SAGE Publications.

Tracy, S. J. (2020). *Qualitative research methods: Collecting evidence, crafting analysis, communicating impact* (2nd ed.). Wiley.

Yin, R. K. (2018). *Case study research and applications: Design and methods* (6th ed.). SAGE Publications.

Chapter 09

Mixed Methods and Triangulation

9.1 Blending Qualitative and Quantitative Approaches.
9.2 Using Triangulation to Enhance Credibility.
9.3 Strategic Applications of Mixed Methods Research.

Mixed methods research is a pragmatic approach that integrates qualitative and quantitative methodologies to address research questions more comprehensively (Creswell & Plano Clark, 2018). This chapter explores the blending of qualitative and quantitative approaches, triangulation to enhance credibility, and strategic applications of mixed methods research in various fields.

9.1 Blending Qualitative and Quantitative Approaches

Mixed methods research combines qualitative and quantitative paradigms to leverage their respective strengths while compensating for their weaknesses.

- Defining Mixed Methods: Mixed methods research involves collecting, analysing, and integrating qualitative and quantitative data within a single study or series of studies (Johnson & Onwuegbuzie, 2004).
- Sequential and Concurrent Designs:

Sequential Designs: One method follows another (e.g., qualitative data informs subsequent quantitative surveys).

Concurrent Designs: Both methods are used simultaneously to triangulate findings (Teddlie & Tashakkori, 2009).

- Strengths of Mixed Methods:

Provides a holistic perspective by addressing both "how" and "why" questions.

Enhances generalizability (quantitative) while capturing rich contextual details (qualitative) (Bryman, 2021).

- Challenges:

Balancing methodological rigour for both paradigms.

Time and resource intensiveness.

For example, a public health study investigating barriers to healthcare access might use qualitative interviews to explore personal experiences and quantitative surveys to measure prevalence and correlations.

9.2 Using Triangulation to Enhance Credibility

Triangulation refers to the use of multiple data sources, methods, theories, or investigators to enhance the credibility and validity of research findings (Denzin, 1978).

- **Types of Triangulation:**

Data Triangulation: Gathering data from different sources (e.g., individuals, groups, or settings).

Methodological Triangulation: Combining qualitative and quantitative methods.

Theoretical Triangulation: Applying multiple theories to interpret data.

Investigator Triangulation: Engaging multiple researchers to analyse data (Patton, 2015).

- **Role in Credibility:** Triangulation reduces researcher bias, strengthens evidence, and ensures findings are not artefacts of a single method or source (Flick, 2018).
- **Case Example:** In disaster management research, triangulating qualitative interviews with satellite imagery and quantitative surveys can provide a nuanced understanding of community resilience.

However, triangulation requires careful planning to ensure coherence between methods and avoid overburdening the study with unnecessary complexity (Yin, 2018).

9.3 Strategic Applications of Mixed Methods Research

Mixed methods research is increasingly applied in interdisciplinary contexts to address complex research problems, inform policy, and guide practice.

- Health Research:

Mixed methods are widely used in public health to evaluate interventions, combining quantitative clinical outcomes with qualitative patient experiences (Creswell & Plano Clark, 2018).

Example: A study on diabetes management might measure HbA1c levels (quantitative) while exploring patients' adherence challenges through interviews (qualitative).

- Education Research:

Mixed methods evaluate teaching strategies by correlating test scores with student and teacher feedback (Tashakkori & Teddlie, 2010).

- Policy Development:

Policymakers use mixed methods to integrate statistical data with community insights, ensuring policies are evidence-based and socially responsive (Greene, 2007).

- Strategic Design Considerations:

Define the priority of qualitative or quantitative methods based on research objectives.

Ensure data integration through frameworks like meta-inference, where insights from both paradigms are synthesised (Bryman, 2021).

Mixed methods approaches are particularly suited to addressing real-world problems that require contextual understanding alongside empirical validation.

Conclusion

Mixed methods research and triangulation are essential for addressing complex research questions, enhancing validity, and informing practice. By blending qualitative and quantitative paradigms, researchers can achieve comprehensive insights, while triangulation ensures methodological rigour and credibility. Strategic applications of these approaches across disciplines highlight their transformative potential in both academic and applied settings.

References

Bryman, A. (2021). *Social research methods* (6th ed.). Oxford University Press.

Creswell, J. W., & Plano Clark, V. L. (2018). *Designing and conducting mixed methods research* (3rd ed.). SAGE Publications.

Denzin, N. K. (1978). *The research act: A theoretical introduction to sociological methods* (2nd ed.). McGraw-Hill.

Flick, U. (2018). *An introduction to qualitative research* (6th ed.). SAGE Publications.

Greene, J. C. (2007). *Mixed methods in social inquiry*. Jossey-Bass.

Johnson, R. B., & Onwuegbuzie, A. J. (2004). Mixed methods research: A research paradigm whose time has come. *Educational Researcher, 33*(7), 14–26.

Patton, M. Q. (2015). *Qualitative research and evaluation methods* (4th ed.). SAGE Publications.

Tashakkori, A., & Teddlie, C. (2010). *Handbook of mixed methods in social and behavioral research* (2nd ed.). SAGE Publications.

Teddlie, C., & Tashakkori, A. (2009). *Foundations of mixed methods research: Integrating quantitative and qualitative approaches in the social and behavioral sciences.* SAGE Publications.

Yin, R. K. (2018). *Case study research and applications: Design and methods* (6th ed.). SAGE Publications.

Chapter 10

Advanced Digital Tools and Techniques

10.1 Using Social Media Analytics for Research.
10.2 Mining Digital Data: Challenges and Opportunities.
10.3 AI and Machine Learning in Qualitative Research

The advancement of digital technologies has significantly transformed research methodologies, enabling novel ways to collect, analyse, and interpret data. This chapter explores three key aspects: the use of social media analytics for research, mining digital data while navigating associated challenges and opportunities, and leveraging artificial intelligence (AI) and machine learning (ML) in qualitative research.

10.1 Using Social Media Analytics for Research

Social media platforms such as Facebook, Twitter, and Instagram provide vast amounts of user-generated content, making them valuable for research.

What is Social Media Analytics?

Social media analytics involves extracting and analysing data from social media platforms to identify patterns, trends, and user behaviours (Kaplan & Haenlein, 2010).

Applications in Research:

Public Health: Researchers use social media data to track disease outbreaks and public sentiment during health crises (Salathé et al. 2012).

Consumer Behaviour: Analysing product reviews and brand mentions to understand market trends (He et al., 2017).

Political Science: Social media sentiment analysis can gauge public opinion on policy issues and election outcomes (Stieglitz et al. 2018).

Tools for Analysis:

Software like Gephi, NodeXL, and social media platforms' APIs allow researchers to collect and visualise data.

Natural Language Processing (NLP) tools analyse sentiment and language patterns (Cambria et al., 2017).

Ethical Considerations:

Issues include user privacy, data consent, and the potential for bias in algorithmic data collection. Researchers must comply with ethical guidelines and platform policies (Zimmer & Kinder-Kurlanda, 2017).

10.2 Mining Digital Data: Challenges and Opportunities

Digital data mining refers to extracting insights from large datasets generated by digital activities, such as web traffic, online transactions, and social interactions.

Opportunities:

Big Data Analysis: Digital data offers unprecedented scale and granularity, enabling insights into societal trends and behaviours (Mayer-Schönberger & Cukier, 2013).

Real-Time Monitoring: Researchers can analyse live data streams, enabling real-time decision-making (Kitchin, 2014).

Cross-Disciplinary Applications: Data mining supports diverse fields, from economics and healthcare to education and environmental science.

Challenges:

Data Quality: Inconsistent or incomplete data can lead to skewed findings. Researchers must implement robust cleaning and preprocessing techniques (Han et al. 2011).

Ethical Concerns: Mining personal data without consent raises privacy issues and can erode public trust. Adherence to data protection laws like GDPR is critical (ICO, 2021).

Technical Complexity: Analysing large datasets requires advanced computational tools and expertise, posing barriers for smaller research teams.

Case Example: A study on online misinformation used machine learning algorithms to mine and classify fake news articles, highlighting the potential of digital data mining to address social challenges (Vosoughi et al., 2018).

10.3 AI and Machine Learning in Qualitative Research

Artificial Intelligence (AI) and Machine Learning (ML) are revolutionising qualitative research by automating data analysis and uncovering complex patterns.

AI/ML in Data Collection:

Chatbots and virtual assistants can conduct interviews or surveys, improving efficiency and accessibility (Araujo et al. 2020).

Social media scraping tools use AI algorithms to collect user-generated content for qualitative studies (Brennen & Kreiss, 2016).

AI/ML in Data Analysis:

NLP tools analyse text for sentiment, themes, and discourse. For instance, Latent Dirichlet Allocation (LDA) can uncover hidden topics in qualitative data (Blei et al., 2003).

Image and video analysis using AI identify visual patterns in multimedia datasets, expanding qualitative research capabilities (Goodfellow et al., 2016).

Advantages of AI/ML in Qualitative Research:

Automates repetitive tasks, saving time.

Enhances accuracy in pattern detection and thematic analysis.

Enables analysis of large-scale qualitative datasets, previously infeasible with traditional methods (Silver & Lewins, 2014).

Ethical and Practical Concerns:

Algorithmic bias can skew results if training data is unrepresentative (Noble, 2018).

The interpretability of ML models poses challenges for qualitative researchers unfamiliar with technical methodologies (Gillespie, 2014).

Case Example: A qualitative study on online activism used AI to analyse millions of tweets, identifying recurring themes and sentiments associated with protest movements (Tufekci, 2014).

Conclusion

Advanced digital tools and techniques have opened new horizons for researchers, particularly in social media analytics, digital data mining, and AI/ML applications. While offering unparalleled opportunities for innovation, these methods also bring challenges related to ethics, technical complexity, and data quality. By adopting these tools responsibly, researchers can enhance the depth, breadth, and relevance of their work in an increasingly digital world.

References

Araujo, T., Helberger, N., Kruikemeier, S., & de Vreese, C. H. (2020). Automated content analysis of news articles: A practical guide. Digital Journalism, 8(4), 496–514.

Blei, D. M., Ng, A. Y., & Jordan, M. I. (2003). Latent Dirichlet Allocation. Journal of Machine Learning Research, 3, 993–1022.

Brennen, J. S., & Kreiss, D. (2016). Digitalization and digitization. International Encyclopedia of Communication Theory and Philosophy. Wiley.

Cambria, E., Schuller, B., Xia, Y., & Havasi, C. (2017). New avenues in opinion mining and sentiment analysis. IEEE Intelligent Systems, 28(2), 15–21.

Goodfellow, I., Bengio, Y., & Courville, A. (2016). Deep learning. MIT Press.

Han, J., Kamber, M., & Pei, J. (2011). Data mining: Concepts and techniques (3rd ed.). Elsevier.

He, W., Zha, S., & Li, L. (2017). Social media competitive analysis and text mining: A case study in the pizza industry. International Journal of Information Management, 33(3), 464–472.

ICO (Information Commissioner's Office). (2021). Guide to the General Data Protection Regulation (GDPR). https://ico.org.uk

Kaplan, A. M., & Haenlein, M. (2010). Users of the world, unite! The challenges and opportunities of social media. Business Horizons, 53(1), 59–68.

Kitchin, R. (2014). Big data, new epistemologies and paradigm shifts. Big Data & Society, 1(1), 1–12.

Mayer-Schönberger, V., & Cukier, K. (2013). Big data: A revolution that will transform how we live, work, and think. Houghton Mifflin Harcourt.

Noble, S. U. (2018). Algorithms of oppression: How search engines reinforce racism. NYU Press.

Salathé, M., Bengtsson, L., Bodnar, T. J., Brewer, D. D., Brownstein, J. S., Buckee, C., ... & Vespignani, A. (2012). Digital epidemiology. PLoS Computational Biology, 8(7), e1002616.

Silver, C., & Lewins, A. (2014). Using software in qualitative research: A step-by-step guide (2nd ed.). SAGE Publications.

Stieglitz, S., Mirbabaie, M., Ross, B., & Neuberger, C. (2018). Social media analytics–Challenges in topic discovery, data collection, and data preparation. International Journal of Information Management, 39, 156–168.

Tufekci, Z. (2014). Big questions for social media big data: Representativeness, validity and other methodological pitfalls. Proceedings of the Eighth International AAAI Conference on Weblogs and Social Media, 505–514.

Vosoughi, S., Roy, D., & Aral, S. (2018). The spread of true and false news online. Science, 359(6380), 1146–1151.

Zimmer, M., & Kinder-Kurlanda, K. E. (2017). Internet research ethics for the social age: New challenges, cases, and contexts. Journal of Empirical Research on Human Research Ethics, 12(1), 1–7.

This draft incorporates foundational concepts, practical applications, and illustrative examples. Let me know if you'd like further refinement or additional details!

SECTION IV

Applications and Implications

Chapter 11

Practical Applications in Various Disciplines

11.1 Marketing and Consumer Research
11.2 Education and Pedagogical Research
11.3 Healthcare and Public Policy Studies
11.4 Social Justice and Advocacy Research

Research methodologies gain value through their application across disciplines, where they inform practice, shape policy, and address societal challenges. Chapter 11 focuses on how research is practically applied in marketing and consumer research, education and pedagogy, healthcare and public policy, and social justice and advocacy.

11.1 Marketing and Consumer Research

Marketing and consumer research has transformed with the rise of data analytics and behavioural science, focusing on understanding consumer behaviour, preferences, and decision-making.

- **Role of Research in Marketing**:

Research is used to develop marketing strategies, optimise product design, and predict market trends (Kotler & Keller, 2016). For instance, customer segmentation studies help brands tailor their offerings to specific demographics.

- **Methods in Practice**:

Quantitative Surveys: Measure consumer preferences and willingness to pay.

Ethnographic Studies: Explore cultural and social influences on consumer behaviour.

Neuromarketing: Uses techniques like eye-tracking and EEG to study subconscious responses to advertisements (Ariely & Berns, 2010).

- **Case Example**: Coca-Cola used social media sentiment analysis to evaluate customer reactions to its "Share a Coke" campaign, allowing real-time adjustments (He et al., 2017).

11.2 Education and Pedagogical Research

Research in education focuses on understanding teaching practices, learning outcomes, and policy impacts.

- **Key Focus Areas:**

Effectiveness of teaching methods.

Equity in education access and outcomes.

The role of technology in enhancing learning experiences.

- **Research Approaches:**

Experimental Studies: Test innovative teaching strategies in controlled environments.

Case Studies: Examine specific schools or communities to identify best practices.

Longitudinal Studies: Track student progress over time to assess the impact of policy interventions.

- **Technological Integration:**

Tools like learning analytics provide insights into student performance, helping educators personalise instruction (Siemens, 2013).

- **Case Example:** A study on flipped classrooms found that students in such environments performed better on assessments and were more engaged in active learning (Bishop & Verleger, 2013).

11.3 Healthcare and Public Policy Studies

Healthcare and public policy research address pressing societal issues, from disease prevention to health equity.

- **Applications in Healthcare:**

Epidemiological studies track disease patterns and inform interventions.

Clinical trials test the efficacy of new treatments.

Behavioural studies explore factors influencing health outcomes (Glasgow et al., 1999).

- **Policy Research:**

Evaluates the impact of public health campaigns and policies.

Uses mixed methods to assess social determinants of health (Bambra et al., 2010).

- **Emerging Tools**:

Digital tools such as electronic health records (EHRs) and AI enable large-scale analyses, improving healthcare delivery and policy planning (Topol, 2019).

- **Case Example**: Research on smoking bans in public spaces demonstrated significant reductions in secondhand smoke exposure and associated health risks, informing similar policies worldwide (Fong et al., 2006).

11.4 Social Justice and Advocacy Research

Research plays a critical role in addressing social injustices, empowering marginalised communities, and influencing advocacy efforts.

- **Focus Areas**:

Investigating systemic inequalities in education, healthcare, and employment.

Documenting the experiences of marginalised groups.

Developing strategies for community empowerment and policy reform.

- **Methodologies in Practice**:

Participatory Action Research (PAR): Involves community members in the research process to ensure findings are actionable and relevant (Chevalier & Buckles, 2013).

Critical Discourse Analysis: Examines how language and communication reinforce power dynamics (Fairclough, 2003).

- **Digital Advocacy**:

Social media platforms amplify voices of advocacy groups and provide real-time data on social movements (Tufekci, 2014).

- **Case Example**: The Black Lives Matter movement utilised research-driven insights to inform campaigns on police reform and racial justice, combining traditional and digital advocacy strategies (Freelon et al., 2016).

Conclusion

The application of research methodologies across disciplines underscores their transformative potential. Whether addressing market dynamics, improving educational outcomes, advancing public health, or promoting social justice, research provides a foundation for evidence-based decisions and impactful interventions. By tailoring approaches to specific disciplinary contexts, researchers can ensure that their work is both relevant and actionable.

References

Ariely, D., & Berns, G. S. (2010). Neuromarketing: The hope and hype of neuroimaging in business. *Nature Reviews Neuroscience, 11* (4), 284–292. https://doi.org/10.1038/nrn2795

Bambra, C., Gibson, M., Sowden, A. J., Wright, K., Whitehead, M., & Petticrew, M. (2010). Tackling the wider social determinants of health and health inequalities: Evidence from systematic reviews. *Journal of Epidemiology & Community Health, 64* (4), 284–291. https://doi.org/10.1136/jech.2008.082743

Bishop, J. L., & Verleger, M. A. (2013). The flipped classroom: A survey of the research. *ASEE National Conference Proceedings.*

Chevalier, J. M., & Buckles, D. J. (2013). *Participatory action research: Theory and methods for engaged inquiry*. Routledge.

Fairclough, N. (2003). *Analysing discourse: Textual analysis for social research*. Routledge.

Fong, G. T., Hyland, A., Borland, R., Hammond, D., Hastings, G., McNeill, A., & Zanna, M. P. (2006). Reductions in tobacco smoke pollution and increases in support for smoke-free public places following the implementation of comprehensive smoke-free workplace legislation in Ireland: Findings from the ITC Ireland/UK Survey. *Tobacco Control, 15*(S3), iii51–iii58. https://doi.org/10.1136/tc.2005.013649

Freelon, D., McIlwain, C. D., & Clark, M. D. (2016). Beyond the hashtags: #Ferguson, #Blacklivesmatter, and the online struggle for offline justice. *Center for Media & Social Impact.*

Glasgow, R. E., Vogt, T. M., & Boles, S. M. (1999). Evaluating the public health impact of health promotion interventions: The RE-AIM framework. *American Journal of Public Health, 89*(9), 1322–1327. https://doi.org/10.2105/AJPH.89.9.1322

He, W., Zha, S., & Li, L. (2017). Social media competitive analysis and text mining: A case study in the pizza industry. *International Journal of Information Management, 33*(3), 464–472. https://doi.org/10.1016/j.ijinfomgt.2013.12.005

Kotler, P., & Keller, K. L. (2016). *Marketing management* (15th ed.). Pearson Education.

Siemens, G. (2013). Learning analytics: The emergence of a discipline. *American Behavioral Scientist, 57*(10), 1380–1400. https://doi.org/10.1177/0002764213498851

Topol, E. J. (2019). *Deep medicine: How artificial intelligence can make healthcare human again*. Basic Books.

Tufekci, Z. (2014). Big questions for social media big data: Representativeness, validity and other methodological pitfalls. *Proceedings of the Eighth International AAAI Conference on Weblogs and Social Media*, 505–514.

Chapter 12

Reporting and Presenting Qualitative Findings

12.1 Writing Reports for Academic and Strategic Audiences.
12.2 Visualising Findings: Infographics, Dashboards, and multimedia.
12.3 Publishing in the Digital Era.

Qualitative research findings are most impactful when communicated effectively. Chapter 12 focuses on writing comprehensive reports, leveraging visual tools to enhance understanding, and adapting to digital publishing formats to ensure accessibility and engagement.

12.1 Writing Reports for Academic and Strategic Audiences

Writing reports for academic and strategic audiences requires tailoring content to suit their specific needs.

Academic Audiences:

Academic reports are often detailed, focusing on theoretical contributions and methodological rigour.

- § *Structure*: Includes a literature review, methodology, findings, and a discussion.
- § *Tone and Style*: Prioritises clarity, objectivity, and adherence to academic writing conventions (Silverman, 2021).
- § *Purpose*: To advance knowledge, contribute to theory, and encourage further research.

Strategic Audiences:

Reports for policymakers, industry leaders, and practitioners emphasise actionable insights and recommendations.

- § *Structure*: Concise executive summaries, key findings, and strategic recommendations.
- § *Tone and Style*: Accessible language, focusing on practical implications (Patton, 2015).
- § *Purpose*: To inform decision-making and inspire change.

Key Considerations in Writing:

- § Transparency in data collection and analysis enhances credibility (Tracy, 2010).
- § Using participant quotes adds authenticity and depth to findings (Saldana, 2016).

Example: A study on workplace diversity might present theoretical models for academic audiences and actionable steps for HR managers in strategic reports.

12.2 Visualising Findings: Infographics, Dashboards, and Multimedia

Visual tools play a critical role in making qualitative findings accessible and engaging.

Infographics:

- § Infographics condense complex information into easily digestible visuals..
- § Ideal for summarising trends, patterns, or thematic insights.
- § Combines text, images, and charts to appeal to non-specialist audiences (Krum, 2014).

Dashboards:

- § Dashboards are interactive tools that provide real-time access to data and findings.
- § Commonly used in fields like public health and business analytics.
- § Facilitate stakeholder engagement by enabling users to explore data dynamically (Few, 2012).

Multimedia Presentations:

- § Incorporating videos, audio clips, and animations can bring qualitative findings to life, especially for ethnographic studies or participatory research.
- § Enhances audience connection by showcasing participant voices and real-life contexts.

Key Principles for Effective Visualisation:

- § Simplicity: Avoid clutter and focus on key messages (Tufte, 2006).
- § Relevance: Tailor visuals to the audience's needs and interests.
- § Accuracy: Ensure visuals faithfully represent the data.

Example: In a study on mental health services, a dashboard might show patterns in service accessibility, while infographics summarise community feedback.

12.3 Publishing in the Digital Era

The Digital Era offers unprecedented opportunities for disseminating qualitative research, but it also presents unique challenges.

Open Access and Online Journals:

Open access platforms make research findings more widely available, fostering global knowledge sharing.

- § Encourages collaboration and cross-disciplinary engagement (Suber, 2012).
- § Challenges include maintaining quality standards and navigating publication fees..

Digital Storytelling:

Combining narrative and technology, digital storytelling uses videos, blogs, and social media to reach broader audiences.

- § Effective for advocacy and community-based research.
- § Engages stakeholders by personalising findings and highlighting lived experiences (Robin, 2008).

Ethical Considerations in Digital Publishing:

- § Protecting participant confidentiality is critical, especially when sharing multimedia content.
- § Researchers must navigate copyright and intellectual property issues (Borgman, 2015).

Emerging Trends in Publishing:

- § *Preprint Servers*: Allow researchers to share findings quickly, fostering timely feedback and discussion.
- § *Interactive Publications*: Include embedded videos, hyperlinks, and data visualisations to enhance reader engagement (Ponte, 2019).

Example: A qualitative study on climate change adaptation could be published as an open access article with supplementary multimedia content, such as interviews and infographics, to engage policymakers and the public.

Conclusion

Reporting and presenting qualitative findings is a multifaceted process that involves tailoring communication strategies to diverse audiences, leveraging visual tools to enhance accessibility, and embracing digital platforms for dissemination. By adopting these practices, researchers can maximise the impact and reach of their work.

References

Borgman, C. L. (2015). *Big data, little data, no data: Scholarship in the networked world*. MIT Press.

Few, S. (2012). *Show me the numbers: Designing tables and graphs to enlighten* (2nd ed.). Analytics Press.

Krum, R. (2014). *Cool infographics: Effective communication with data visualization and design*. Wiley.

Patton, M. Q. (2015). *Qualitative research and evaluation methods* (4th ed.). Sage.

Ponte, D. (2019). The future of interactive academic publishing. *Journal of Scholarly Publishing, 50*(2), 87–102. https://doi.org/10.3138/jsp.50.2.87

Robin, B. R. (2008). Digital storytelling: A powerful technology tool for the 21st-century classroom. *Theory Into Practice, 47*(3), 220–228. https://doi.org/10.1080/00405840802153916

Saldana, J. (2016). *The coding manual for qualitative researchers* (3rd ed.). Sage.

Silverman, D. (2021). *Qualitative research* (5th ed.). Sage.

Suber, P. (2012). *Open access*. MIT Press.

Tracy, S. J. (2010). Qualitative quality: Eight "big-tent" criteria for excellent qualitative research. *Qualitative Inquiry, 16*(10), 837–851. https://doi.org/10.1177/1077800410383121

Tufte, E. R. (2006). *The visual display of quantitative information* (2nd ed.). Graphics Press.

Chapter 13

Future of Qualitative Research

13.1 Trends Shaping the Future of Digital Qualitative Methods.
13.2 Addressing the Challenges of Digital Research.
13.3 Towards a More Inclusive and Global Research Framework.

Qualitative research continues to evolve as new technologies and global challenges reshape its landscape. Chapter 13 explores emerging trends in digital qualitative methods, addresses the challenges inherent in digital research, and highlights the movement towards a more inclusive, global research framework.

13.1 Trends Shaping the Future of Digital Qualitative Methods

Advancements in technology and societal shifts are driving innovation in qualitative research methods.

[a] Integration of AI and Machine Learning

Artificial intelligence (AI) is transforming qualitative research by automating processes like coding and thematic analysis. Machine learning algorithms identify patterns in vast data sets, allowing researchers to focus on interpretation (Silverman, 2021). For example, natural language processing (NLP) tools analyse text data from interviews or social media.

[b] Rise of Virtual Ethnography.

Virtual ethnography, or "netnography," adapts traditional ethnographic methods to online communities. Researchers observe and interact with participants on social media platforms, forums, or virtual worlds, expanding access to diverse populations (Kozinets, 2019).

[c] Emergence of Mixed Digital Media

Multimedia tools, such as video diaries, digital storytelling, and augmented reality, are being increasingly incorporated to capture rich, context-sensitive data (Pink et al. 2016).

[d] Advancing Visualisation Techniques

Interactive dashboards, AI-driven visualisations, and immersive tools like virtual reality (VR) are used to present findings dynamically, making research accessible to broader audiences (Tufte, 2006).

[e] Ethical Implications.

Emerging digital tools raise ethical questions about privacy, consent, and data ownership. Researchers must navigate these challenges while adhering to rigorous ethical standards (Buchanan & Zimmer, 2018).

13.2 Addressing the Challenges of Digital Research

While digital methods offer significant benefits, they also pose unique challenges that researchers must address.

Data Overload

The ease of collecting digital data can lead to overwhelming volumes of information. Researchers need effective strategies for data management, such as utilising AI tools or structured coding frameworks (Flick, 2018).

Ethical Dilemmas in Digital Contexts

- *Informed Consent*: Ensuring participants fully understand how their data will be used, especially in passive data collection from social media or apps.
- *Anonymity and Confidentiality*: Protecting identities in environments where personal information is easily traceable.
- *Digital Divide*: Ensuring equitable access to participation for marginalised groups with limited digital literacy or connectivity (Markham & Buchanan, 2012).

Technological Bias and Accessibility

Digital tools often reflect biases embedded in their design, which can influence data interpretation. Researchers must critically assess the tools they use and ensure their work remains inclusive and accessible (Noble, 2018).

Reliability of Online Data

With misinformation prevalent online, researchers face challenges in verifying the authenticity of digital data. Triangulation and validation methods become critical in addressing this issue (Patton, 2015).

Security and Data Protection

As cyber threats grow, qualitative researchers must adopt robust data security measures to safeguard sensitive information. Encryption and compliance with data protection regulations like GDPR are essential (Van den Eynden et al., 2011).

13.3 Towards a More Inclusive and Global Research Framework

The future of qualitative research is increasingly characterised by efforts to decolonise methodologies and foster inclusivity.

Decolonizing Qualitative Research:

Researchers are challenging Eurocentric paradigms by incorporating indigenous knowledge systems and participatory approaches that value local perspectives (Smith, 2012). This shift ensures that research is culturally relevant and respects the autonomy of marginalised communities.

Global Collaboration and Knowledge Sharing:

Digital platforms enable researchers from diverse contexts to collaborate and share findings. Open access journals, virtual conferences, and online repositories democratise knowledge dissemination (Suber, 2012).

Inclusivity in Participant Recruitment:

Efforts to include underrepresented voices, such as those from low-income countries or minority groups, are essential for generating comprehensive insights. Researchers are leveraging digital tools to overcome geographical and logistical barriers (Bennett & Checkoway, 2011).

Adaptation to Global Challenges:

Climate Change Research: Qualitative methods are vital in understanding community responses and adaptive practices (Leach et al. 2018).

Health Equity: Researchers are exploring the social determinants of health to address disparities in global healthcare (Bambra et al. 2010).

Digital Transformation: As societies digitise, qualitative research provides insights into the human dimensions of technological change.

Example Initiatives:

The Global South Research Partnership encourages equitable collaboration between researchers in high-income and low-income countries.

Participatory action research (PAR) empowers communities to co-create solutions to local problems, bridging gaps between research and practice (Chevalier & Buckles, 2013).

Conclusion

The future of qualitative research is shaped by rapid technological advancements, ethical challenges, and a growing emphasis on inclusivity and global perspectives. By embracing innovative digital tools, addressing challenges head-on, and prioritising equity, qualitative researchers can contribute to solving complex global issues.

References

Bambra, C., Gibson, M., Sowden, A. J., Wright, K., Whitehead, M., & Petticrew, M. (2010). Tackling the wider social determinants of health and health inequalities: Evidence from systematic reviews. *Journal of Epidemiology & Community Health, 64* (4), 284–291. https://doi.org/10.1136/jech.2008.082743

Bennett, T., & Checkoway, B. (2011). Inclusive participatory research for social justice. *American Behavioral Scientist, 56*(10), 1415–1425. https://doi.org/10.1177/0002764211433796

Buchanan, E. & Zimmer, M. (2018). Internet research ethics. *The Stanford Encyclopedia of Philosophy*. Retrieved from https://plato.stanford.edu/entries/ethics-internet-research/

Chevalier, J. M., & Buckles, D. J. (2013). *Participatory action research: Theory and methods for engaged inquiry*. Routledge.

Flick, U. (2018). *An introduction to qualitative research* (6th ed.). Sage.

Kozinets, R. V. (2019). *Netnography: The essential guide to qualitative social media research* (3rd ed.). Sage.

Leach, M., Scoones, I., & Stirling, A. (2018). Governing epidemics in an age of complexity: Narratives, politics, and pathways to sustainability. *Global Environmental Change, 25*(1), 58–68. https://doi.org/10.1016/j.gloenvcha.2014.02.005

Markham, A., & Buchanan, E. (2012). Ethical decision-making and Internet research. *AOIR Ethics Working Committee*. Retrieved from https://aoir.org/ethics/.

Noble, S. U. (2018). *Algorithms of oppression: How search engines reinforce racism*. NYU Press.

Pink, S., Horst, H., Postill, J., Hjorth, L., Lewis, T., & Tacchi, J. (2016). *Digital ethnography: Principles and practice*. Sage.

Silverman, D. (2021). *Qualitative research* (5th ed.). Sage.

Smith, L. T. (2012). *Decolonizing methodologies: Research and indigenous peoples* (2nd ed.). Zed Books.

Suber, P. (2012). *Open access*. MIT Press.

Tufte, E. R. (2006). *The visual display of quantitative information* (2nd ed.). Graphics Press.

Van den Eynden, V., Corti, L., Woollard, M., Bishop, L., & Horton, L. (2011). Managing and sharing data: Best practices for researchers. UK Data Archive.

SECTION V

Computer-Assisted Qualitative Data Analysis Software (CAQDAS)

Chapter 14

Software for Qualitative Data Analysis

14.1 NVivo v.14 (2023 version): Step-by-Step Exploration
14.2 QDA Miner
14.3 Taguette
14.4 Thematic.ai
14.5 MAXQDA
14.6 ATLAS.ti
14.7 QualCoder
14.8 Hyper Research
14.9 Content analysis.
14.10 Qualtrics XM
14.11 Hubspot
14.12 Text analysis
14.13 Weft Qualitative Data Analysis.
14.14 RQDA
14.15 F4analysis

Computer-Assisted Qualitative Data Analysis Software (CAQDAS) has revolutionised qualitative research by offering powerful tools to organise, analyse, and visualise complex datasets. This section explores key CAQDAS options, focusing on their features, applications, and limitations, providing researchers with a comprehensive guide to choosing the most appropriate software for their needs from the following lists.

14.1 NVivo v.14 (2023 Version) Step-by-Step Applications

NVivo is among the most widely used CAQDAS platforms due to its versatility and robustness in handling qualitative data. The 2023 version, NVivo v.14, includes updates in collaboration tools and AI-assisted coding.

Key Features

- § Importing multiple data types, including interviews, social media data, and surveys.
- § Visual tools like word clouds and network maps.
- § AI features for automated coding and thematic analysis (QSR International, 2023).

Applications

Used in diverse fields, including healthcare, social sciences, and marketing, for exploring relationships in text, audio, and video data.

Limitations

- § High cost.
- § Requires steep learning curve.

Example: A researcher exploring mental health discussions on Twitter can use NVivo to categorise tweets by themes and generate visualisations of emerging patterns.

14.1.1 NVivo Qualitative Analysis Software: A Comprehensive Analysis

NVivo is a leading computer-assisted qualitative data analysis software (CAQDAS) designed to aid researchers in organising, analysing, and visualising qualitative data. Developed by QSR International, NVivo has become an essential tool for academic, professional, and market researchers across various disciplines. This essay explores NVivo in detail, including its step-by-step applications, strengths, weaknesses, cost-benefit analysis, sources of acquisition and cost, and maintenance considerations.

1.0 Step-by-Step Applications of NVivo

NVivo offers a structured approach to managing and analysing qualitative data, enabling researchers to derive insights efficiently.

1.1 Data Import

The first step involves importing data into the software. NVivo supports multiple formats, including text (Word, PDF), audio, video, images, and datasets from Excel or SPSS.

Example: A researcher studying mental health blogs can import text and multimedia files to analyse sentiment and themes.

1.2 Data Organisation

Researchers organise imported data using nodes, which represent themes or categories. NVivo offers two primary types:

Tree Nodes: Hierarchical structures for thematic analysis.

Case Nodes: Categorisation based on individual entities or cases.

1.3 Coding Data

Coding involves tagging text, audio, or video segments with relevant nodes. NVivo's AI-assisted features suggest potential codes, reducing manual effort.

1.4 Analysing Data

NVivo provides tools for:

Word Frequency Analysis: Identifying commonly used words.

Query Functions: Examining relationships and trends in data.

Visualisations: Creating word clouds, cluster maps, and network diagrams.

1.5 Generating Reports

Finally, NVivo allows researchers to export analysis results into comprehensive reports, facilitating publication or presentation.

2.0 Strengths of NVivo

2.1 Versatility

NVivo supports diverse data formats, including interviews, focus groups, and survey responses, making it suitable for various research disciplines (Bazeley & Jackson, 2013).

2.2 Advanced Analytical Tools

Features such as sentiment analysis, automated coding, and data visualisation enhance the depth and quality of analysis (Edwards-Jones, 2014).

2.3 Scalability

NVivo can handle large data sets, making it ideal for projects requiring extensive data analysis.

2.4 Collaboration Capabilities.

The latest versions support cloud-based collaboration, enabling research teams to work simultaneously on the same project.

2.5 Integration with Other Platforms

NVivo integrates with tools like Microsoft Word, Excel, and reference managers (e.g., EndNote), streamlining workflows.

3.0 Weaknesses of NVivo

3.1 High Cost

NVivo's licensing cost is a significant barrier for individual researchers and smaller institutions (Zamawe, 2015).

3.2 Steep Learning Curve.

While powerful, NVivo's interface and functionalities require substantial training to use effectively.

3.3 Resource Intensity

NVivo requires high computational resources, limiting accessibility for users with older hardware.

3.4 Limited Support for Real-Time Analysis

Although NVivo integrates well with static datasets, it lacks robust tools for analysing real-time data streams like live social media feeds.

4.0 Cost-Benefit Analysis

4.1 Costs

Initial Costs:

- § Academic licences for NVivo start at approximately USD 124 annually for students and USD 670 for professionals (QSR International, 2023).
- § **Training Costs:**
- Workshops or online training sessions may cost an additional USD 100–300.
- § **Maintenance Costs:**
- Annual updates or technical support fees are sometimes required, depending on the licence type.

4.2 Benefits

- § **Time Savings:**
- Automated features like sentiment analysis and text search queries reduce manual coding time.
- § **Improved Data Insights:**
- NVivo's robust analytical tools enable deeper understanding and better publication outcomes.
- § **Collaboration and Scalability:**
- Cloud-based collaboration increases team efficiency, particularly for interdisciplinary projects.

4.3 Cost Effectiveness

For large-scale or multi-year research projects, the benefits often outweigh the costs. Institutions and funded projects gain the most value due to higher utilisation rates.

5. Sources of Acquisition and Costs

NVivo can be purchased directly from QSR International's website or authorised resellers. Pricing varies based on user type and region.

5.1 Individual Licences

Student Licences: USD 124/year for academic use.

Professional Licences: USD 670/year or USD 1,150 for perpetual licences.

5.2 Institutional Licences

Custom pricing for academic or organisational site licences, typically based on the number of users.

5.3 Free Trial

QSR International offers a 14-day free trial, allowing researchers to evaluate the software before purchase.

6. Maintenance

6.1 Technical Support

QSR International provides extensive online support through documentation, webinars, and technical help desks.

6.2 Updates and Upgrades

Minor Updates: Included in annual subscriptions.

Major Version Upgrades: Often require additional fees for perpetual licence holders.

6.3 Compatibility Requirements

Maintaining up-to-date hardware and software systems ensures optimal performance. Minimum requirements for NVivo v.14 include:

8 GB RAM (16 GB recommended).

Windows 10/MacOS 11 or higher.

Conclusion

NVivo remains a cornerstone tool in qualitative research due to its comprehensive features, advanced analytics, and versatility. Despite its high cost and learning curve, the software delivers exceptional value for large-scale, interdisciplinary, or complex projects. Researchers must weigh the software's strengths against its limitations to determine its suitability for their specific needs.

References

Bazeley, P., & Jackson, K. (2013). *Qualitative data analysis with NVivo* (2nd ed.). Sage.

Edwards-Jones, A. (2014). Qualitative data analysis with NVivo. *Journal of Education for Teaching, 40* (2), 193–195. https://doi.org/10.1080/02607476.2013.866724

QSR International. (2023). *NVivo qualitative data analysis software.* Retrieved from https://qsrinternational.com

Zamawe, F. C. (2015). The use of NVivo software for qualitative data analysis: An overview. *Malawi Medical Journal, 27*(1), 36–38.https://doi.org/10.4314/mmj.v27i1.9

14.2 QDA Miner

QDA Miner excels in mixed methods research, allowing for the integration of qualitative and quantitative analysis.

Key Features:

Statistical analysis tools.

Supports geotagged data and open-ended survey responses.

Applications:

Ideal for projects requiring text analysis alongside numeric data.

Limitations:

Limited multimedia support (Provalis Research, 2023).

14.3 Taguette

Taguette is an open-source CAQDAS designed for beginner-friendly qualitative research.

Key Features:

Cloud-based collaboration.

Intuitive tagging system for thematic coding.

Applications:

Suitable for educators and small research teams working on textual data.

Limitations:

Limited support for multimedia files (Rampin et al., 2023).

14.4 Thematic.ai

Thematic.ai is an AI-powered platform for customer feedback analysis.

Key Features:

Automated theme detection using machine learning.

Integration with survey platforms like Qualtrics.

Applications:

Widely used in marketing and customer experience research.

Limitations:

Focused on textual analysis; limited for broader qualitative projects (Thematic.ai, 2023).

14.5 MAXQDA

MAXQDA offers robust tools for data visualisation and qualitative data management.

Key Features:

Interactive document and video coding.

Integration with mixed methods tools like SPSS.

Applications:

Suitable for academic and professional projects in social sciences and humanities (VERBI Software, 2023).

Limitations:

Expensive licensing.

14.6 ATLAS.ti

ATLAS.ti is renowned for its user-friendly interface and comprehensive analytics.

Key Features:

Powerful visualisations like network maps.

Multilingual text analysis.

Applications:

Used extensively in large-scale academic and industrial research projects (Scientific Software Development GmbH, 2023).

Limitations:

High learning curve and cost.

14.7 QualCoder

QualCoder is a free, open-source CAQDAS that supports thematic coding and analysis.

Key Features:

User-defined coding categories.

Multimedia analysis support.

Applications:

Suitable for independent researchers or students.

Limitations:

Limited advanced analytics compared to paid options (Gibbs, 2018).

14.8 HyperRESEARCH

HyperRESEARCH is a versatile platform for qualitative analysis with a focus on multimedia data.

Key Features:

Multimedia annotation.

Cross-platform compatibility.

Applications:

Useful in fields like anthropology and media studies.

Limitations:

Limited visualisation tools.

14.9 Content Analysis

Content analysis tools focus on extracting meaning from textual data systematically.

Key Features:

Quantitative and qualitative coding.

Frequency analysis.

Applications:

Effective for media and political communication studies (Neuendorf, 2017).

Limitations:

Labour-intensive setup.

14.10 Qualtrics XM

Qualtrics XM combines survey design with basic text analytics.

Key Features:

Integration of quantitative and qualitative responses.

Text sentiment analysis.

Applications:

Popular in business and customer satisfaction research (Qualtrics, 2023).

Limitations:

Limited depth for qualitative-only projects.

14.11 HubSpot

HubSpot integrates CRM tools with customer feedback analysis.

Key Features:

Social media monitoring.

Customer feedback sentiment analysis.

Applications:

Effective for qualitative insights in marketing campaigns.

Limitations:

Restricted to customer interaction data.

14.12 Text Analysis

General text analysis tools apply to diverse qualitative research.

Key Features:

Sentiment analysis and keyword extraction.

Works with open-source libraries like Python's NLTK.

Applications:

Cross-disciplinary use for linguistic and thematic research.

14.13 Weft Qualitative Data Analysis

Weft is a free, open-source tool for coding and retrieval of qualitative data.

Key Features:

Simple text coding.

Cross-platform support.

Applications:

Ideal for small-scale projects.

Limitations:

Limited advanced features.

14.14 RQDA

RQDA is a lightweight, R-based qualitative analysis tool.

Key Features:

Integrates with R for statistical analysis.

Open-source.

Applications:

Ideal for mixed methods researchers familiar with R (Huang, 2016).

Limitations:

Requires technical expertise.

14.15 F4analysis

F4analysis focuses on transcription and analysis of qualitative data.

Key Features:

Time-coded transcription tools.

Intuitive interface.

Applications:

Used in interview-based research.

Limitations:

Minimal visualisation features.

Conclusion

The growing range of CAQDAS platforms provides researchers with powerful tools to enhance qualitative research. Researchers can streamline analysis and produce robust, meaningful insights by selecting the appropriate software based on project needs.

References

Gibbs, G. R. (2018). *Analysing qualitative data* (2nd ed.). Sage.

Huang, R. (2016). RQDA: An R-based tool for qualitative data analysis. *R Journal, 8*(1), 80–89.

Kozinets, R. V. (2019). *Netnography: The essential guide to qualitative social media research* (3rd ed.). Sage.

Neuendorf, K. A. (2017). *The content analysis guidebook* (2nd ed.). Sage.

Provalis Research. (2023). *QDA Miner*. Retrieved from https://provalisresearch.com

QSR International. (2023). *NVivo v.14*. Retrieved from https://qsrinternational.com

Qualtrics. (2023). *Qualtrics XM*. Retrieved from https://qualtrics.com

Rampin, R., & Contributors. (2023). *Taguette: Your qualitative research assistant*. Retrieved from https://taguette.org

Scientific Software Development GmbH. (2023). *ATLAS.ti*. Retrieved from https://atlasti.com

Thematic.ai. (2023). *Thematic.ai platform*. Retrieved from https://getthematic.com

VERBI Software. (2023). *MAXQDA 2023*. Retrieved from https://maxqda.com

Chapter 15

Extended Qualitative Research Methodologies

15.1 Means-End Chain Theory
15.2 Laddering Technique.
15.3 Kelly Repertory Grid
15.4 Online Qualitative Methods

The extended qualitative research methodologies delve into the detailed processes, examples from the literature, suitable applications, strengths, weaknesses, and strategies to overcome these challenges are addressed in this chapter.

15.1 Means-End Chain Theory

The Means-End Chain (MEC) theory is a framework used in qualitative research to explore the connections between product attributes, the benefits derived from those attributes, and the personal values they fulfil. It helps researchers understand consumer decision-making processes by focusing on how individuals perceive the utility of a product in fulfilling their life goals or values (Gutman, 1982; Reynolds & Gutman, 1988). This approach assumes that choices are driven by a hierarchical relationship that progresses from attributes to consequences and, finally, to values.

Process

1. **Identify the Research Focus:** Define the product, service, or experience to be analysed.
2. **Data Collection:** Conduct in-depth interviews using a laddering technique (discussed below) to uncover relationships between attributes, benefits, and values.
3. **Content Analysis:** Identify common themes and relationships among the collected responses.
4. **Construct Hierarchical Value Maps (HVMs):** Organise the data into a visual representation that links attributes to consequences and values.
5. **Interpretation and Application:** Use insights to inform marketing strategies, product design, or consumer behaviour research.

Notable Contributors

- Gutman (1982) laid the groundwork for MEC theory, highlighting its application in understanding consumer choice behaviour.
- Reynolds and Gutman (1988) formalised the use of laddering interviews to link attributes to higher-order values.
- Pieters et al. (1995) applied MEC theory to advertising to understand how consumers relate to advertisements based on values.

Suitable Situations

- Analysing consumer purchasing behaviour and preferences.
- Developing targeted marketing or advertising campaigns.
- Designing new products that align with consumer values.

Strengths

- Provides a deep understanding of consumer motivations.
- Helps link functional benefits to psychological and emotional factors.
- Facilitates the development of tailored marketing strategies.

Weaknesses

- Requires skilled interviewers and participants comfortable with abstract discussions.
- Time-intensive data collection and analysis process.
- Risk of researcher bias in interpreting hierarchical relationships.

Overcoming Challenges

- Use standardised protocols and training for interviewers to ensure consistency.
- Employ software tools for data analysis to reduce subjectivity.
- Cross-validate findings with quantitative data to enhance reliability.

15.2 Laddering Technique

Laddering is an in-depth qualitative interview method often used alongside MEC theory. It systematically explores the reasons behind consumer choices by delving into a hierarchical sequence from attributes to consequences and then to values (Reynolds & Gutman, 1988). By asking a series of "why" questions, laddering uncovers the underlying motivations and cognitive structures influencing decision-making.

Process

1. **Define Research Objectives:** Clearly outline the purpose of the study and the product or service being analysed.
2. **Recruit Participants:** Select a representative sample of consumers.

3. **Conduct Interviews:**

- Begin with open-ended questions about preferences or experiences.
- Use iterative "why" questions to explore the connections between attributes, benefits, and values.

4. **Data Transcription:** Document responses verbatim for analysis.
5. **Analyse Responses:** Categorise attributes, consequences, and values.
6. **Map Hierarchies:** Visualise relationships to identify patterns.

Notable Contributors

- Reynolds and Gutman (1988) established laddering as a method for applying MEC theory.
- Gengler and Reynolds (1995) refined laddering for use in marketing and consumer research.
- Grunert et al. (2001) used laddering to study food consumption behaviours.

Suitable Situations

- Investigating consumer decision-making in detail.
- Exploring the psychological and emotional drivers behind product preferences.
- Informing product development and branding strategies.

Strengths

- Provides rich, qualitative insights into consumer behaviour.
- Encourages participants to reflect on their choices and values.
- Supports the development of meaningful and resonant marketing messages.

Weaknesses

- Time-consuming for both interviews and analysis.
- Participants may feel fatigued or uncomfortable with repetitive "why" questions.
- Subjectivity in data interpretation can lead to inconsistent results.

Overcoming Challenges

- Train interviewers to build rapport and minimise discomfort.
- Limit the number of questions to avoid participant fatigue.
- Use software tools for organising and analysing qualitative data.

15.3 Kelly Repertory Grid

The Kelly Repertory Grid (KRG) method, developed by George Kelly in 1955, explores individual perceptions and constructs by identifying and comparing elements (Kelly, 1955).

Constructs refer to the dimensions people use to interpret and differentiate elements in their environment. The method allows researchers to understand subjective experiences and cognitive frameworks.

Process

1. **Define Elements:** Identify the objects, events, or people relevant to the research question.
2. **Elicit Constructs:** Ask participants to compare and contrast elements to identify underlying constructs.
3. **Rate Elements:** Use a grid format to rate elements based on elicited constructs.
4. **Analyse Data:** Examine patterns, clusters, or themes in the constructs to uncover unique perspectives.

Relevant Literature

- Kelly (1955) introduced the repertory grid as part of his *Personal Construct Theory.*
- Jankowicz (2004) discussed its applications in organisational and business contexts.
- Tan and Hunter (2002) used the repertory grid to analyse management decision-making processes.

Suitable Situations

- Exploring individual perceptions and cognitive structures.
- Understanding decision-making processes in complex environments.
- Investigating personal or organisational identity.

Strengths

- Captures unique, individual perspectives.
- Adaptable to diverse research contexts, including psychology and organisational studies.
- Generates structured, analyzable data.

Weaknesses

- High cognitive demand on participants to articulate constructs.
- Requires significant time for data collection and analysis.
- Limited comparability across participants.

Overcoming Challenges

- Simplify instructions and provide examples to guide participants.
- Use software tools for efficient data analysis.
- Combine KRG with complementary methods for validation.

15.4 Online Qualitative Methods

Online qualitative methods leverage digital platforms to collect data through interviews, focus groups, surveys, and ethnographic studies. The rise of digital technology and the COVID-19 pandemic has popularised these methods for remote and asynchronous research (Gray et al., 2020; Kozinets, 2015).

Process

1. **Select Platform:** Choose tools like Zoom, Microsoft Teams, or online survey software.
2. **Design Study:** Define objectives, recruit participants, and prepare interview or survey questions.
3. **Data Collection:** Conduct virtual interviews, focus groups, or ethnographic observations.
4. **Transcription:** Record and transcribe sessions for analysis.
5. **Analyse Data:** Apply thematic or content analysis to identify patterns and themes.

Notable Contributors

- Kozinets (2015) detailed methods for online ethnography in *Netnography.*
- Hamilton and Bowers (2006) explored the use of online focus groups in healthcare research.
- Gray et al. (2020) discussed the advantages of online qualitative research during the COVID-19 pandemic.

Suitable Situations

- Research involving geographically dispersed participants.
- Studies exploring online behaviours or digital communities.
- Situations where physical interactions are impractical (e.g., during pandemics).

Strengths

- Cost-effective and time-efficient.
- Broad reach, enabling access to diverse participant groups.
- Flexibility in data collection through asynchronous or synchronous methods.

Weaknesses

- Technology barriers for some participants.
- Loss of non-verbal cues during virtual interactions.
- Ethical concerns about privacy and data security.

Overcoming Challenges

- Provide training or technical support to participants unfamiliar with digital tools.
- Use video conferencing to capture non-verbal communication.
- Ensure robust data encryption and adherence to ethical standards.

Conclusion

Each of these qualitative research methods provides unique tools for exploring human behaviour, perceptions, and motivations. While they offer rich insights, their successful implementation depends on careful planning, skilled execution, and addressing potential limitations. Combining these methods with quantitative approaches can further enhance the validity and applicability of research findings.

References

Gray, L. M., Wong-Wylie, G., Rempel, G. R., & Cook, K. (2020). Expanding qualitative research interviewing strategies: Zoom video communications. *International Journal of Qualitative Methods*, 19, 1–9.

Gengler, C. E., & Reynolds, T. J. (1995). Consumer understanding and advertising strategy: Analysis and strategic translation of laddering data. *Journal of Advertising Research*, 35(4), 19-33.

Grunert, K. G., Grunert, S. C., & Sørensen, E. (2001). Means-end chains and laddering: Theoretical background and practical guidelines. *International Journal of Research in Marketing*, 20(1), 1-16.

Gutman, J. (1982). A means-end chain model based on consumer categorisation processes. *Journal of Marketing*, 46(2), 60-72.

Hamilton, R. J., & Bowers, B. J. (2006). Internet recruitment and e-mail interviews in qualitative studies. *Qualitative Health Research*, 16(6), 821-835.

Chapter 16

Preference of Qualitative Research Methodology Over Quantitative and Mixed Methods

16.1 Qualitative Versus Quantitative Research
16.2 Qualitative vs. Mixed Methods
16.3 Strengths and Weaknesses of Qualitative Research Methodology
16.4 Strategies to Address Weaknesses
16.5 Examples of Well-Known Qualitative Research Projects

16.1 Qualitative Versus Quantitative Research

Qualitative research emphasises understanding human experiences, behaviours, and social phenomena through exploration and interpretation. Unlike quantitative research, which focuses on numerical data and statistical analysis, qualitative research prioritises depth over breadth (Creswell & Poth, 2018). This makes it especially valuable for answering questions about "how" and "why" events or behaviours occur.

16.1.1 Key Reasons for Preferring Qualitative Research

1. **Rich and Detailed Data**

Qualitative methods allow for in-depth exploration of complex phenomena, capturing the nuances of human experiences (Denzin & Lincoln, 2018). For instance, ethnographic studies delve into the cultural and social contexts that shape behaviours, which quantitative surveys often overlook.

2. **Flexibility**

Unlike quantitative research, which follows a rigid structure, qualitative methodologies are adaptive. Researchers can modify questions or focus areas as new themes emerge during data collection.

3. **Subjective Insights**

Qualitative research excels at understanding individual perspectives, beliefs, and emotions, providing insights into how people interpret their realities (Patton, 2015). This is essential in fields like psychology and anthropology.

4. **Exploratory Nature**

In situations where little is known about a phenomenon, qualitative research serves as a foundational step to identify themes and generate hypotheses. For example, exploratory studies on new social media platforms often begin with qualitative methods.

5. **Contextual Understanding**

Qualitative research is particularly effective in understanding behaviours within specific cultural, historical, or social contexts where numerical data alone cannot provide a full picture.

16.1.2 Limitations of quantitative research in contexts where qualitative research excels

- Numerical data often fail to capture the depth of human experiences, reducing complex phenomena into simplistic metrics (Bryman, 2016).
- Quantitative methods are less effective in exploring dynamic or emergent phenomena where hypotheses have not yet been formed.

16.2 Qualitative Versus Mixed Methods

Mixed methods combine qualitative and quantitative approaches, offering comprehensive insights. However, qualitative research alone is preferred in certain contexts due to the following:

1. **Focus on Depth Over Breadth**

Mixed methods can dilute the depth achieved by qualitative approaches. In cases where detailed, context-specific insights are needed, qualitative research is more appropriate.

2. **Resource Efficiency**

Mixed methods often require significant resources, including expertise in both quantitative and qualitative techniques. For smaller projects or when resources are limited, qualitative methods are more practical.

3. **Theoretical Development**

When the goal is to develop new theories rather than test existing ones, qualitative research is typically more suitable (Creswell & Poth, 2018).

4. **Reducing Complexity**

Mixed methods can become overly complex, making it harder to draw clear conclusions. In contrast, qualitative research maintains focus and simplicity, especially for exploratory studies.

16.3 Strengths and Weaknesses of Qualitative Research Methodology

16.3.1 Strengths of Qualitative Research

1. **Depth and Richness**

Qualitative research captures detailed narratives and experiences, providing a nuanced understanding of human behaviour (Patton, 2015).

2. **Context-Specific Insights**

By focusing on specific cultural, social, or historical settings, qualitative methods reveal how context influences behaviour and decision-making (Denzin & Lincoln, 2018).

3. **Adaptability**

Researchers can adjust methodologies in response to emerging findings, making qualitative research particularly suited for dynamic or poorly understood phenomena.

4. **Exploration of Subjectivity**

Qualitative methods prioritise participants' perspectives, offering insights into emotions, beliefs, and motivations that cannot be quantified (Creswell & Poth, 2018).

5. **Theoretical Contribution**

Grounded theory and other qualitative methods allow researchers to build new frameworks or theories based on empirical data.

6. **Inclusive of Marginalised Voices**

Qualitative research often emphasises giving voice to underrepresented or marginalised populations, fostering equity in research (Bryman, 2016).

16.3.2 Weaknesses of Qualitative Research

1. **Subjectivity**

The reliance on researcher interpretation can introduce bias, affecting the validity and reliability of findings.

2. **Time-Consuming**

Data collection (e.g., interviews, focus groups) and analysis (e.g., thematic coding) require significant time and effort.

3. **Limited Generalizability**

Findings from qualitative studies are often specific to the context and may not be applicable to other populations or settings.

4. **Smaller Sample Sizes**

Qualitative research typically involves fewer participants, limiting the representativeness of the findings.

5. **Challenges in Replication**

The uniqueness of qualitative studies makes them difficult to replicate, affecting reliability (Bryman, 2016).

16.4 Strategies to Address Weaknesses

- **Subjectivity:** Use inter-coder reliability and triangulation to minimise bias.
- **Time-Consuming Nature:** Leverage qualitative data analysis software (e.g., NVivo, ATLAS.ti) to streamline coding and analysis.
- **Limited Generalizability:** Combine qualitative insights with quantitative methods in mixed methods designs.
- **Small Sample Sizes:** Focus on theoretical saturation to ensure the depth and validity of findings.
- **Replication Challenges:** Maintain transparent documentation of research design, data collection, and analysis processes.

16.5 Examples of Well-Known Qualitative Research Projects

16.5.1 The Chicago School of Urban Sociology

- **Context:** During the early 20th century, the Chicago School conducted ethnographic studies on urban environments.
- **Methodology:** Participant observation and in-depth interviews.
- **Key Contributions:** William Whyte's *Street Corner Society* (1943) provided groundbreaking insights into the social structures of urban Italian-American communities.

16.5.2 Clifford Geertz's Balinese Cockfight Study

- **Context:** Geertz's seminal ethnographic work explored cockfighting in Bali as a form of symbolic communication.
- **Impact:** His interpretive approach emphasised the role of culture in shaping behaviour (Geertz, 1973).

16.5.3 Paulo Freire's Pedagogy of the Oppressed

- **Context:** Freire explored literacy among marginalised communities in Brazil.

- **Methodology:** Participatory research, where participants were actively involved in shaping the research process.
- **Impact:** Advocated for critical pedagogy, emphasising empowerment and dialogue in education (Freire, 1970).

16.5.4 UK Biobank Ethics Studies

- **Context:** While primarily a quantitative project, qualitative studies explored participants' views on genetic data sharing.
- **Impact:** Provided insights into public trust and ethical considerations in biobanking research (Kaye et al., 2012).

16.5.5 Netnography in Digital Behaviour Studies

- **Context:** Robert Kozinets developed netnography to study online communities.
- **Methodology:** Online ethnographic observations of digital interactions.
- **Impact:** Provided a framework for understanding consumer behaviour in digital spaces (Kozinets, 2015).

16.5.6 The "Seven Up" Longitudinal Documentary Series

- **Context:** This UK-based project followed the lives of 14 children from various socio-economic backgrounds over several decades.
- **Methodology:** Long-term qualitative observation and interviews.
- **Impact:** Offered profound insights into the influence of class and opportunity on life trajectories.

16.5.7 Studying HIV/AIDS Narratives in South Africa.

- **Context:** Researchers used life history interviews to explore the stigma and challenges faced by people living with HIV/AIDS.
- **Impact:** Shed light on cultural and social barriers to treatment, informing public health interventions.

Conclusion

Qualitative research offers unparalleled depth and contextual understanding, making it invaluable for exploring human behaviour and social phenomena. While it has limitations, such as subjectivity and limited generalisability, these challenges can be addressed through methodological rigour and complementary approaches. Well-known qualitative projects, such as Geertz's cultural studies and the Chicago School's urban sociology, highlight the transformative impact of this methodology on our understanding of complex issues.

References

Bryman, A. (2016). *Social research methods* (5th ed.). Oxford University Press.

Creswell, J. W., & Poth, C. N. (2018). *Qualitative inquiry and research design: Choosing among five approaches* (4th ed.). Sage Publications.

Denzin, N. K., & Lincoln, Y. S. (Eds.). (2018). *The Sage handbook of qualitative research* (5th ed.). Sage Publications.

Freire, P. (1970). *Pedagogy of the oppressed.* Herder and Herder.

Geertz, C. (1973). *The interpretation of cultures: Selected essays.* Basic Books.

Kaye, J., Curren, L., Anderson, N., et al. (2012). Ethical implications of the use of genetic data in biobanking research. *European Journal of Human Genetics, 20*(9), 879–882.

Kozinets, R. V. (2015). *Netnography: Redefined.* Sage Publications.

Patton, M. Q. (2015). *Qualitative research & evaluation methods* (4th ed.). Sage Publications.

About the Author

Dr. Samuel Adeyinka-Ojo has an extensive academic and professional background in different disciplines. He holds a BSc (Hons) in Accounting and a Postgraduate Diploma in Marketing [PGDM]. Sam holds an MBA in Marketing, an MBA in General Management, a Master of ICT Management, and an MSc in Public Health and Health Promotion from Brunel University of London, United Kingdom. He studied for a Graduate Certificate in Business [GCB] (International Business) from Monash University Australia and a PhD in Hospitality and Tourism from the prestigious Taylor's University in Malaysia. Samuel was the first African ever to graduate from Taylor's University (TU) with a PhD degree. He was also awarded a Post-Crisis Hospitality Management Certificate and a DEI Certificate from the University of South Florida, USA. He is a member of the Chartered Institute of Marketing [MICIM] (UK) and an associate member of the Chartered Management Institute, UK. He has been awarded a Senior Fellow of the Higher Education Academy, United Kingdom, a Member of the Australian Institute of Project Management (MAIPM), a Member of the Australian Marketing Institute (MAMI), a Certified Management and Business Educator (CMBE) of the Chartered Association of Business Schools, UK, and a Certified Member of the Project Management Institute, USA. He has worked in several companies as a sales manager, business development manager, and marketing manager in the downstream sector of the oil and gas industry. He was the Head of Department (HOD) of Marketing (2017-2019) and HOD of Management, Marketing, and Digital Business (2021-2023), and a Senior Lecturer at the Faculty of Business, Curtin University Malaysia. He teaches undergraduate programmes and project management modules for M.Sc. degree in project management and Master of International Business modules. As a digital and strategic qualitative researcher, he has supervised HDR (MPhil and PhD) and M.Sc. by coursework students to completion. He consulted for the Sarawak State Government, Malaysia, on staff training on Industry 4.0 in 2020 and the Greater Miri Development Master Plan 2030 (Tourism Cluster). He has won several university and international awards in education leadership, teaching, and learning. He has contributed to and participated in community engagement services and CSR initiatives.

www.ingramcontent.com/pod-product-compliance
Ingram Content Group UK Ltd.
Pitfield, Milton Keynes, MK11 3LW, UK
UKHW062008290726
14090UKWH00022B/1452

9 798896 324775